R. G. Rossom
22

TWAYNE'S WORLD AUTHORS SERIES

A Survey of the World's Literature

Sylvia E. Bowman, Indiana University

GENERAL EDITOR

AUSTRALIA

Joseph Jones, University of Texas

EDITOR

Henry Lawson

(*TWAS* 133)

TWAYNE'S WORLD AUTHORS SERIES (TWAS)

The purpose of TWAS is to survey the major writers—novelists, dramatists, historians, poets, philosophers, and critics—of the nations of the world. Among the national literatures covered are those of Australia, Canada, China, Eastern Europe, France, Germany, Greece, India, Italy, Japan, Latin America, New Zealand, Poland, Russia, Scandinavia, Spain, and the African nations, as well as Hebrew, Yiddish, and Latin Classical literatures. This survey is complemented by Twayne's United States Authors Series and English Authors Series.

The intent of each volume in these series is to present a critical-analytical study of the works of the writer; to include biographical and historical material that may be necessary for understanding, appreciation, and critical appraisal of the writer; and to present all material in clear, concise English—but not to vitiate the scholarly content of the work by doing so.

Henry Lawson

By A. A. PHILLIPS

Wesley College
Melbourne, Australia

Twayne Publishers, Inc. :: New York

Library of Congress Catalog Card Number: 71–110708

MANUFACTURED IN THE UNITED STATES OF AMERICA

Preface

It is usual, in a book such as this, for the author to analyze in turn each of the works of the writer whom he is discussing. Such an approach to Henry Lawson would be inappropriate, because that work consists entirely of short stories, prose sketches, and ballad verse. The volumes which he published contain collections of such material and thus lack unity of theme.

I have therefore preferred to devote each chapter of this book to a different aspect of Lawson's work or of his relationship to the Australian community of his time. Consequently, the same piece of his writing may here be examined several times from differing points of view.

Lawson's significance as a writer partly depends on his reflection of specifically Australian attitudes and of the developing Australian cultural nationalism which marked his period. I have therefore begun my discussion with an attempt to indicate the outlook of the Australian community at the time when Lawson was establishing his reputation as an affectionately acclaimed exponent of its ideology.

In a previous work—*The Australian Tradition*—I have recorded many of my opinions about Lawson's work. Since readers of the present work are unlikely to be familiar with the earlier one, I have incorporated here several passages from it. I am grateful to the Lansdowne Press for permission to make these citations. I am also indebted to Messrs. Angus and Robertson for permission to quote many passages from the works of Lawson, and two from Joseph Furphy's *Such is Life* and Miles Franklin's *My Brilliant Career*, respectively.

Contents

Chronology

1867	June 17, Henry Lawson born at Grenfell, New South Wales.
1870	Family moves to Eurunderee.
1883	Lawson goes to Sydney; works as a coach-painter.
1887	First printing of verses in *The Bulletin,* Sydney.
1890	Employed as journalist on the Brisbane *Boomerang.*
1892	Journeys through the country west and north of Bourke.
1893	First visit to New Zealand; working as manual laborer.
1894	Mother issues a small volume of his prose and verse.
1896	Angus and Robertson issue *In the Days When the World Was Wide* (verse) and *While the Billy Boils* (prose). Marriage to Bertha Bredt.
1897	The Lawsons are appointed to direct the Maori School at Mangamaunu, New Zealand.
1898	Jim Lawson born. The Lawsons return to Sydney.
1900	Bertha Lawson born. The Lawsons go to London.
1901	Two volumes by Lawson published in England.
1902	The Lawsons return to Australia. Hannah Thornburn dies. Henry and Bertha separate.
1910	At Mallacoota.
1911	Professor Saillens' French translations of Lawson's stories published in Paris.
1916	At the Yanco Irrigation Settlement. A dramatized version of stories presented in Sydney.
1922	September 2, Henry Lawson dies at Sydney.

CHAPTER 1

The Australians of the Nineties

IF ONE uses the phrase "the Nineties" in an English context, one suggests the picture of willowy esthetes bewailing, or celebrating, the decadence of a dying century. Use the same phrase in an Australian context, and one calls up the image of callous-palmed he-men, contemptuous of collars and refinement, confronting the future with a brash self-confidence. The decade has acquired something of the status of legend in the national self-assessments of the Australian people—as the title of the best book about the period indicates.[1] It was the time when the tiny group of colonists realized that they had tamed, within a century, a forbidding continent; they realized, too, that they had developed a society and a human type marked by their own character—and vastly superior, in their view to the played-out communities of Europe. They had begun to see themselves as the architects of a revitalizing Utopia which would give practical shape to the egalitarian conceptions of the Enlightenment. They were already showing a readiness to attempt sociopolitical experiments; they were touchily resentful of the patronizing attitude of the English; and they were beginning to develop a literature reflective of the special character of the people, and expressive of its ambitions and its ideology.

The general character of this community is not difficult for the American observer to understand, for it is expressive of the "frontier spirit" which so strongly influenced American life—Australian usage prefers the term "Outback" to "Frontier," but the spiritual connotations of the two words are much the same. Yet the parallel can be misleading, for there are important differences between the two communities—Sydney Webb, the English social analyst, visiting both countries in 1898, found the contrasts between them more significant than their likenesses.[2] For example, the Australians had no traditions of violence, save that which may have lingered from the convict settlements. They were independent, brash, contemptuous of official ukase and decorous social convention. They liked to entertain themselves with fist-fights: certain bushrangers had attained the status of folk heroes: but the bushman's social creed did not sanction the use of firearms to settle private disputes, lynchlaw was almost unknown, and the mining camps impressed observers by their orderliness, enforced by popular will rather than by official constraints.

There was a more significant difference in the measure of influence exercised by the frontier spirit in the two countries. In the United States—at least as it is imaged by such an outsider as I, with only a desultory knowledge of American history—the frontier spirit was essentially a counterforce importantly modifying the influences emanating from the great commercial centres, but ultimately less determinative than they of the character of the nation. In Australia, the frontier spirit was a dominant gene, as it were. Certainly the cities led in such activities as political maneuver or the shaping of the educational system, but they did not determine the human spirit or the moral values of the community. It was generally recognized that the "Bush" was the "Real Australia," the environment in which the special qualities of the Australian as a human type were evolving.

In Lawson's story "Telling Mrs. Baker" a city girl—a very nice one—has been present at an incident in which two bushmen display the finer qualities of their kind. Afterward she exclaims "I like the bushmen. They are grand men—they're noble." [3] That was the kind of recognition which Australian sentiment of the nineties would expect from a nice city girl.

Such generalizations, of course, tell less than the complete truth. Often enough the Australian townsman felt the usual urban scorn for rustic crudity. But he did often acquiesce in the belief that the bushman had an innate superiority and also believed that the qualities of this type had become engraved on the national character, so that the townsman shared them too. Certainly, the bushman had little doubt of the justice of his claim to a moral superiority. Like the cowboy or gaucho, he saw himself as marked by a superior virility, independence, wholesomeness and sense of reality.

I *The Australian Conviction of Superior Reality*

This belief in the superior grasp of reality of the Australian is well conveyed in a letter sent by an early migrant, James Henty, writing in 1831 to his brother in England: "Colonising is enough to bring any man to his senses: it unveils the mist by which (from the artificial state of things) every man is more or less encompassed in England. It compels a man to think and act for himself." [4]

That sentiment would have commanded very general Australian assent. The bushman, indeed, found in the challenge of the harsh environment by which he was faced something of the quality which Joseph Conrad found in the sea. It confronted a man with an ineluctable test, before which the evasions, or the pretenses, practiced by the landsman, or the townsman—and which could produce the illusion of success—were ineffective. Only real strength, a mastered skill, and stamina could ensure victory, or even survival. The cowboy, no doubt, believed much the same, but, faced by the more complex currents of a more developed and a more varied community, he could not so easily impose a conviction parallel to the bushman's belief that he represented "the True Australian"; and he could not make the bushman's demand that the emerging nation should incorporate in its ethos his dominant sense of values.

II *Belief in the Common Man*

There was a difference, too, in the form taken by the egalitarian impulses of the two nations. Both strongly believed in the value of democratic impulses. Both scorned the class stratifications of the European societies, the pretensions of the European upper classes and the overready servility of the European proletariat. Both were equally devoted to the "man's a man for a' that" conception. But to the American the fundamental condition on which the achievement of democracy rested was that of Equality of Opportunity. Provided the society was able to assure that condition, he accepted the idea of the pursuit of success by pre-eminence over others, particularly economic pre-eminence, under conditions which deliberately emphasized competitive motivations. As the American saw it, democracy was working well if one could fairly claim, in a parody of Napoleon's phrase, that every backwoodsman carried a tycoon's checkbook in his bedroll.

Early Australians had largely held the same ideas. It was a country in which it was fairly easy for a man to make his way with little capital and less education. As with America, too, there was a secondary ideal of assuring to the little man the chance of a smallholder's sturdily modest independence. A long battle had been fought to "unlock the Land," largely pre-empted by large pastoral holders. The radicals had fought their Land Laws onto the Statute Book, but the practical results had been disappointing. By the nineties, the chance of upward economic movement for the small man was much less, although it was still much greater than in Europe. Australian sentiment began to swing away from the "American Dream" which it had hitherto shared. It acquired a patriotism of the working class. It did not merely reject the idea of capitalist competition as the desirable basis of an adventurous society. Nor was its attitude merely a defensive mechanism against the possessors' oppression—although such battles were vigorously fought. There was a positive side to the sense of working-class solidarity, a confidence that the economic underdog was in fact a better man than his nominal superior. Australia, like America, had largely been created by men who had escaped from the dark Satanic mills of the European slums, or the more endurable, but scarcely less mean, servility of still feudal villages. Such men had found in the conditions of the new countries a chance to prove their individual worth as men. They were intoxicated by the sense of achievement and self-confidence which the new countries allowed to the common man. That feeling was perhaps more widespread in Australia than in America because it was not diluted by a highly developed industrialization, with its inevitable accompaniment of a sense of human alienation.

Furphy, greatest of Australian novelists, explains the source and the nature of this form of bushman's pride in a passage in which he is attacking the snob-romantics of certain English novelists working in Australia, who assumed in their work the mystic superiority of the man of "blood and breeding":

> Urbane address, faultless syntax, even that good part which shall not be taken away, namely, the calm consciousness of inherent superiority, are of little use here. And yet your Australian novelist finds no in-

consistency in placing the bookish student, or the city dandy, many degrees above the bushman or the digger, or the pioneer, in vocations which have been the life-work of the latter. . . . And what an opportunity for some novelist, in his rabid pursuit of originality, to merely reverse the incongruity—picturing the semi-barbarian, lassoed full-grown, and launched into polished society, there to excell the fastidious idlers of drawing-room and tennis court in their own line! This miracle would be more reasonable than its antitheses. Without doubt it is easier to acquire gentlemanly deportment than axeman's muscle; easier to criticise an opera than to identify a beast seen casually twelve months before; easier to dress becomingly than to make a bee-line, straight as the sighting of a theodolite, across strange country in foggy weather; easier to recognise the various costly vintages than to live contentedly on the smell of an oiled rag.

. . . And it is surely time to notice the threepenny braggadocio of caste which makes the languid Captain Vernon de Vere (or words to that effect) an overmatch for half-a-dozen white savages, any one of whom could take his lordship by the ankles and wipe the battlefield with his patrician visage . . . , which makes a party of resourceful bushmen stand helpless in the presence of fire and flood, till marshalled by some hero of the croquet lawn; above all which makes the isocratic and irreverent Australian fawn on the "gentleman" for no imaginable reason except that the latter says "deuced" instead of "sanguinary," and "by Jove" instead of "by sheol." [5]

This working-class loyalty and sense of confidence in their essential superiority partly issued in a somewhat truculent avoidance of anything which might seem like submissiveness to an employer, and a rejection of the middle class's claim to cultural leadership. English visitors in the nineteenth century were shocked to observe that the Australian workingman did not touch his hat to the boss. This attitude slopped over into a general hostility to authority. As I have said, the community was an exceptionally orderly one, but its members were determined exponents of the "one word from you and I do as I like" outlook. The bushrangers, except for those of an exceptionally brutal type, could usually count on a stream of information about the whereabouts of the troopers. Much of it came from men who were quite law-abiding themselves but who had an emotional sympathy with rebellion. I have always seen as characteristic of my countrymen a couple who fell into conversation with me at a football match. They were a pleasant, easy-natured pair, who, one felt sure, would hurry to the help of a neighbor in trouble and feed heaps of cookies to their children's playmates. Yet when the wife rose to hoot the referee from the arena at halftime, her whole body shook with passion. I felt that she was engaged in a cathartic ritual, compressing into it the expression of the antiauthoritarian posture enjoined upon her by the national outlook, so that for the rest of the week she was free to practice the relaxed friendliness, which is also typical of her people.

III *Socialism without Doctrines*

This proletarian bushman's pride issued in the dominant political creed of the country, which has been aptly described as "Socialism without Doctrines." Of course, the Radical doctrines were accepted and vigorously preached—particularly those of Henry George who had a very strong Australian following. But the Australian temperament is markedly pragmatic. That belief in the superior feeling for reality of the Australian issued in a certain scorn of "isms." The brief century of Australian development had been dominated by the need to subdue the difficult and empty continent, a task in which sweat achieved more than ideas. It gave rise to the Australian's strong belief in the practical. It is notable that of those Australians who have achieved international intellectual eminence, most have been scientists; there has been only one philosopher of note, and he was a Jew born in the country. Of the artists who are known outside their own country, most have been singers or painters; there are fewer writers and, as yet, no composers (with one possible exception). That order accurately reflects the Australian preference for the concrete over the abstract. Hence, in politics the nation was more concerned with the implementation of practical reform than with the framing of manifestos —despite the fact that the radicalism of the nineties had a strong flavor of Utopianism, centered round the conviction that Australia was destined to show the world the way of escape from capitalist sin.

Trade unionism and a Labour Party organization supporting it had strongly developed during the eighties. Early in the nineties the movement suffered two crushing defeats, when large-scale strikes, on the waterfront and in the wool-shearing sheds, collapsed in failure. Popular opinion attributed these defeats largely to the support given to the employers' cause by governments controlled by Conservatives and judicial benches manned by lawyers with a middle-class background. The radical leaders therefore determined that success in the industrial struggle needed the capture of the institutions of government, and they therefore turned their attention to political organization. Popular opinion flowed strongly with them—so much so, that by 1904 a Labour Party Prime Minister headed the Commonwealth government. With success, inevitably came moral erosions—through the practical politician's necessary reliance on compromises, and through opportunists who used the party to attain the flesh-pots which accompany the exercise of power. In the nineties, however, the movement was strongly idealistic, and had the emotional force of aspiration. It felt a large confidence in the future, as yet little touched by experience of the corrupting influence of achieved power. The Australian proletarians were traveling hopefully, or, rather, with brash confidence.

IV *Mateship*

It will be seen that the watchwords of Liberty and Equality strongly influenced the attitudes of the time, although the Australians preferred to use less abstract and less pretentious terms. Fraternity, the third term in the classic trinity, had an even stronger appeal, and there was an even stronger tendency to substitute for it a more homely term. As the bushman felt it, loyalty to one's comrades was the very basis of manly virtue. Indeed he was so naïvely convinced that it was specifically an Australian virtue that he invented for it his own term, Mateship. He usually spelled it with a capital letter—a distinction which he would hardly have accorded to honor or love or mercy. Radical agitators were quick to make use of this deification. "Socialism is only Mateship" they would declaim, knowing the emotional response which could be roused by this slogan.

A digression is suggested at this point. Australians have developed only a few words of their own, far fewer than the Americans. When, therefore, they do find a need to evolve their own term for some human quality, it strongly suggests that the quality has for them a particular importance related to their sense of the nature of the national character. Thus it is worth noticing that "a fair go" was evolved to give the conception of justice a more concrete and democratic flavor. The epithet "dinkum" is less easily translatable. It suggests a mixture of staunchness, sincerity, bluntness, and the Conradian sense of realism, the kind of comfortable, frank reliability which a bushman looked for in his mate. The word "skite" (equals "boaster") is more ambiguous. It may reflect the realist's scorn for mere words as inferior to the proof of action, or it may indicate awareness of a national weakness for self-assertiveness.

It is perhaps fitting that Australians preferred the term Mateship to Fraternity, for their practice of the virtue was narrowly conceived. They were an intensely nationalistic community; it does not seem to have occurred to them that this attitude contradicted the Socialistic ideology which they had adopted. They were liable to boast that they were "99% British," which, they smugly assumed, was somehow a guarantee of virtue. Not that they highly regarded the English, save when some outsider attacked them.

V *Attitudes to Non-Australians*

There is little need to expand on their attitude toward the English, for it was very similar to, and had the same ambivalences as, the contemporary American attitude. There was the same resentment of the English tendency to patronize the cultural immaturities of the young countries, the same conviction that those young countries had a more virile and a more democratic outlook than England, and the same underlying sense of affectionate regard for the source of their Anglo-Saxon mores—the same exasperated contradictions as those felt by a restive teen-ager who loves his parents, but finds them intolerably fusty. The one important difference was that there was no widespread desire in Australia to break the political tie with England—for both sentimental and practical reasons.

For all foreigners, the Australians felt a lofty contempt untouched by any real knowledge of them, save for the Americans, for the Australians already felt that the two peoples shared a common outlook. Xenophobia was particularly strong toward all Asiatics. This largely rested on economic fears: Australians did not want to see their high level of wages broken down by the competition of men used to a much lower standard of living. The White Australia doctrine was not fully imposed until the achievement of Federation in 1901, but it was already strongly advocated and partly enforced. Feeling was particularly strong against the Chinese who had entered the country in some numbers during the Gold Rushes. They were suspected of all sorts of dark vices, suspicions which had no relation to the orderly, good-natured industriousness of the Chinese in the country. In this form of prejudice, however, Australians did not differ much from other communities of European stock.

As yet, too, Australians felt only the mildest tremors of guilt for their destructive treatment of the continent's aborigines. On the whole, they assumed that the Blacks were a primitive lot, who had had perforce to give way to superior civilization in the interests of progress; and they did not look too closely at the methods by which the near-extinction of the aborigines had been achieved, or the moral basis on which the white seizure of the continent rested. In the Australians' comfortable sense of superiority to the lesser breeds without the law, then, one can perceive a naïvely unrecognized paradox. They felt that they could justly look down on others, partly because they thought that they were so much better at the practice of Mateship and democracy.

This brief sketch of the outlook of the nineties is misleading at one point at least. It suggests a people much given to sentimentally romantic idealism, and this is, in a sense, true; yet it inaccurately conveys the atmosphere of the people. They made something of a fetish of a roughness of manners. They practiced an ironic approach to life, a tight-lipped laconic realism. The tone is suggested by a favorite story of World War I. An Anzac went out into no man's land to rescue a friend who had been wounded (a not uncommon expression of the doctrine of Mateship). He slung the wounded man over his shoulder and started back for his own lines under enemy fire. The wounded man protested, "Eh, Mate, how about carrying me the other way round? This way, you're gettin' the Victoria Cross and I'm gettin' the bullets."

VI *The Mythic Element*

It may also be objected that what I am presenting is the way the Australians of the nineties saw themselves, rather than the way they really were. That is fair criticism; the kind of simplified generalizations in which I have summarized my picture will not contain the complex truth. Thus it is fair to suggest, as I have done, that dominant Australian sentiment supported radical political ideas; but the Labour Party by no means always won elections, least of all in those electorates where the bushmen voted. The men who looked forward to the Australian victory over the evils of capitalism also adventured their spare pennies in speculation in mining stock, a favorite occupation with all classes of the community.

To distinguish between what the Australian thought he was and what he really was would be an impossible task, for, of course, there was no such thing as the Australian—only some four million Australians, of whom few were identical twins. It is also not very relevant to my present purpose. What I have been attempting to suggest is the nature of the Australian "myth" of the nineties. Myths, even in the special sense in which I am using the term, do not always conform to facts, but they matter none the less; for what a people believe they are, they tend to become. The medieval knights did not behave according to the chivalric idealisms which Malory depicted; but the myth of chivalry was a more important influence on European culture than the actual behavior of the knights. To establish some sense of the nature of the myth has a particular importance to my present purpose of introducing a writer who was the inheritor and, in some measure, the interpreter of that myth.

VII *"The Bushman's Bible"*

The myth had its most forceful expression in *The Sydney Bulletin,* a weekly newspaper of marked originality and vitality, and of immense popular appeal. It had been founded in the early eighties by J. F. Archibald, a kindly, industrious, shrewd journalist-of-vocation, who appeared to sustain life on the smell of printer's ink. He was not a man of much personal ambition, no newspaper tycoon hungry for power on the Harmsworth model; but he had a clear and tenaciously held vision of the kind of Australia he wanted, and he gradually evolved a clear idea of the kind of paper which could help to create it. He was no personal genius with the pen. Hard work and a talent for skilful sub-editing were his most obvious talents; and, more importantly, he had a flair for spotting men of talent, and when he had scooped them in, he could command their loyalty.

From the beginning Archibald set out to address an audience of the "True Australians" as the myth interpreted that term. He declared that he aimed his paper at "the very salt of the Australian people, the educated independent mining prospector." [6] He thus narrowly specified his audience because it happened that he had more experience of the mining camps than of other Outback communities. He could therefore thus best form a concrete picture of his auditor, as a good journalist should; but he used this individualized picture to give imaged form to the wider audience he was aiming at—the bushmen, whether they were cattle drovers, woolshearers, wheat growers, gold prospectors, or, for that matter, townsmen who had adopted the national attitudes which had been incubated in the bush. The paper acquired the proud nickname of "The Bushman's Bible."

The Bulletin was nonetheless a city-produced paper, necessarily very concerned with what was going on there; and perhaps more strongly influenced by a certain reaction against metropolitan influences. The Sydney "Establishment" of the time was not an attractive institution. It was vulgar, smug, and materialistic, and it tried to give a semblance of solidity to its pretensions by apeing all things English—upper-class English, that is. Its members jostled and thrust for the attention of the English aristocrat who occupied Government House. It was probably the most unattractive feature of contemporary Australian life, and it stood for all that Archibald's "independent prospector" rejected. *The Bulletin* set out to destroy its influence, and at the same time to stir the metropolis out of a lethargic indifference to ideas. Hence its earlier numbers, particularly, have a certain street-Arab quality—a compulsive eagerness to bung a lump of road metal whenever a top hat heaves in sight. As the paper matured, Archibald developed, and more strongly emphasized, a positive expression of Australian nationalism, working out a detailed sociopolitical policy, although for fifty years *The Bulletin* remained cheerfully and cheekily eager to outrage the conventions of bourgeois respectability.

The first page of the Christmas number for 1887 illustrates both the cocky iconoclasm and the embryonic development of an Australian radical policy. It is devoted to a piece of rough-and-ready verse in which *The Bulletin* declares itself (mock modesty was never one of its failings). I quote some of the more informing passages:

We've managed some reforms and will continue
To work out more according to our lights:
We'll biff out bigger frauds, with manlier sinew,
Made harder by a hundred punier fights.
We're ready now to let out straight and win you
At least a small percentage of your rights. . . .

We're ready for 'em, singly or in batches,
The priest who prays to eat nor eats to pray,
Whose fat, large claw, whate'er his creed be, snatches
From pallid meagreness its food away!

We're dead against the lash and mean to scourge it
And its high priests with our own little thong.
Can brutalism uplift our race or purge it
Of vice, or violence, or doing wrong?

We're for Home Rule . . .
. . . Nor it
Alone, but in Time's lordlier fullness we
Will knit our millions in a shining nation
A later, manlier, freer Federation.

We're for Land Tax, and not another tax on
The face of earth. Men have too long been blind,
Too long the patient workful Anglo-Saxon
Has wrought for lustier idlers of his kind.
We love not the foul Mongol: this we've shown in
Our recent utterances; he must go. . . .

What else? Oh, lots of things! Whatever turns up
That doesn't look like truth, we'll go for straight!
We'll break some idols, tip some sacred urns up,
And hurt some corns, we guess and calculate:
And from where Etna's dreadful column burns up
To Nova Zembla, we will educate
All men to freedom (we were brought up meekly),
And all of this for only sixpence weekly!

The following page is less rambunctious—it is the leader page. It opens with a Christmas effusion, but it is hardly in the best Dickensian Yuletide tradition:

One thousand eight hundred and eighty-seven years ago tomorrow was born in Bethlehem of Judea that Jesus whose life and teaching were to furnish forth a new inspiration to man and a new moral basis to the world's social civilisation. . . . . and if Jesus tomorrow came to keep his birthday with the world for which he has done so much, he would be arrested as a Fenian, hanged as an anarchist in Chicago, sent to Siberia as a Nihilist, hunted, hounded down, cursed, bayoneted and trampled under foot, for the world to-day knows not Jesus.

The second leader is an attack on alleged English imperialist aims in Australia, with a side blast at the Sydney Establishment:

The bait is carefully disguised; those who profferred it well know the snobbish imbecility by which Australia is governed . . .

Each of these leaders is about 1,500 words long. The argument is often closely reasoned and is backed by an informed knowledge of history. The comparative solidity of this matter suggests a revealing contrast.

Archibald's working-class audience was in a sense provided for him by the Compulsory Education Acts of the seventies. Contemporaneously, Harmsworth (later Lord Northcliffe) had realized the existence of a lower-class audience in England created by similar legislation at about the same time. He set out to exploit it, assuming that these lowly fellows who had learned how to read would be incapable of thinking. He therefore gave them, in his paper *Answers*, a diet of pap—scraps and shreds never more than a few lines long, demanding the minimum of concentrated attention. Archibald trusted that his bushman audience would welcome an invitation to think, although he was careful to spice the bait with plenty of pugnacious rhetoric. The resounding success of his paper indicates that he had rightly estimated the quality of the men he admired.

Not that Archibald by any means despised the short paragraph. He provided plenty of them; but they were usually shrewdly devised to support his iconoclastic aims. Thus the same number contains a passing gibe:

Mary Anderson won't come to Australia without her Ma's protection. Mary needn't be so much afraid. We have no Royal Highnesses here, except King Billy of Gum Flat, and he never visits theatres.

The target of the gibe is, of course Edward, Prince of Wales, whose amorous eclecticism was the subject of universal gossip—which was never reported in respectable organs of the British press. A later paragraph is perhaps more significant:

> The usual daily outrage story is to hand . . . and on the strength of it, four young men stood the usual chance of being hanged on the testimony of the Mary Jane Hicks of the occasion, a nice-looking girl in tears. The only drawbacks to the innocent young creature's story were that she had been assaulted in the same way once or twice before, that she had cohabited with a sea-captain, and that she acknowledged under cross-examination to having held the hat on three occasions while the four abandoned youths drew lots for her. The case was dismissed, but neither magistrate nor policeman dreamed of having the charming young thing arrested for perjury . . .

This is not only a good example of the colorful vigor of style, unconcerned with the nice restraint of literary elegance, which *The Bulletin* had developed. It also conveys something of the tone of the community, the earthy realism which scorned Victorian sentimental conventions. It is notable that *The Bulletin* does not here choose to stand on the high moral ground of an even-handed justice; it is humanly concerned to get a "fair go" for four sinful young rips.

In 1887 Archibald had not yet developed one of the most interesting uses to which he put the short paragraph, as a way of developing his aim of making his readers his contributors. He invited paragraphs from all and sundry. They poured in from all over the country, and the sub-editors brushed up the spelling and grammar, and—more importantly—cut down the amateurs' prolixity to the terse meatiness which Archibald favored. A later feature of the paper particularly devised for these contributors—the "Aboriginalities" page—was devoted to items of bush lore. Hard-bitten outbackers bent unaccustomed fingers round the stubs of pencils to argue about how the young of the kangaroo were born or to enumerate the various ingenious uses which a bushman could find for an empty beer bottle.

VIII *The Bulletin and Australian Literature*

Another purpose of Archibald's, his ambition to create an Australian school of writing, was beginning to bear fruit in 1887. Before *The Bulletin* came on the scene, there can hardly be said to be an Australian literature. A few novels had appeared, mainly written by expatriate Englishmen with an English approach. There were some lyric poets, most of them servilely imitating the nineteenth-century English form of Romanticism. There was a fairly strong body of "folk song," produced by anonymous amateurs and popularized by oral tradition; simple though it was, it had a marked individuality. From this developed the "bush-balladists," men who signed and printed straightforward swinging verses dealing with bush themes. But there was no strong and continuous flow of work with an Australian character.

Archibald understood that if the burgeoning sense of achieved nationhood was to be strongly developed, as he hoped, it would need the support, not only of the political federation for which he was fighting, but of an individual national literature, giving to popular feeling the solidification of an articulate expression. He therefore set out to develop it by seeking out promising writers, throwing his paper open to their work, and nursing them along by his encouragement. He was not a man of highly developed literary taste—his test of a good poem was that "it made your scalp tingle." [7] He met this limitation by seeking out a man who had the qualifications he lacked and installing him as Literary Editor. His own main value lay in the personal encouragement he gave in a kindly, homely fashion which suited the tone of this grass-roots community. If he saw promise in a contribution, "Answers to Correspondents" would suggest that its author should call round sometime at the office. The kind of advice he was likely to get has been described by one with good cause to know:

> Every man has at least one story in him. Some more. . . . Write as simply as you can. . . . Don't strain after effect. . . . Write carefully and write only when you have something to tell the people. How are you off? What are you doing for a living? Are you hard up? Have you got your fare back? Well, if you like, you can go down stairs to Mr.— (the manager or cashier) and I dare say they'll fix you up. Good-bye old man . . .[8]

The 1887 Christmas number, at which we have been glancing, carries a surprising amount of "creative" writing, considering that *The Bulletin* was a weekly newspaper and propaganda sheet, rather than a magazine. There are two short stories, one of them Edward Dyson's "The Golden Shanty" (here bearing a different title), a story which still regularly appears in representative Australian anthologies. There is much verse, most of it not of high quality. Archibald's eagerness to discover and encourage talent is indicated by the Editorial note which heads some verses on "The Wreck of the Castle Derry":

> In publishing the subjoined verses, we take pleasure in stating that the writer thereof is a boy of 17 years and is earning his living under some difficulties as a housepainter—a youth whose poetic genius here speaks eloquently for itself.

Reading "The Derry Castle," one is inclined to be amused at the pitch of Archibald's enthusiasm, even allowing for the greater freedom with which the term "genius" was then used. It seems very much the sort of thing one might expect from a lively-minded youngster whose scalp tingles when he reads poetry, and who determines to have a shot at writing it himself. It shows considerable ability in the use of words and some sensitivity of feeling but there does not seem much to distinguish it from the work of hundreds of young fellows who feel the same impulse and never grow into effective writers.

One would be wrong. Archibald's nose for talent was scenting surely; for the signature on those verses reads "Henry Lawson." Within a decade he was to be affectionately known throughout the continent, and translators would be at work making his stories available to French and German readers.[9]

CHAPTER 2

Biographical Background

WHEN the immense wealth of gold beneath the soil of southeast Australia was revealed in the 1850's, there was the usual wild rush of adventurous optimists. Towns were denuded of tradesmen; graziers found themselves without shepherds; sailors "jumped ship" as they touched at Australian ports. One of these last was a Norwegian youth named Peter Herzberg Larsen.

Little has been discovered about his Norwegian background or his early years in Australia. By 1866 he was at Pipeclay (which was shortly afterward rechristened Eurunderee, the name given to the place by the aborigines) in southern New South Wales: a discovery of gold had been made there not long before. Here Peter Larsen decided to try his hand at a venture no less speculative than gold mining; he married Louisa Albury, an eighteen-year-old working in her father's combined shanty and shop. As things turned out, it was no lucky strike for Peter.

Within a year, the couple moved on—with some 10,000 others—to a newly opened gold field at Grenfell. Here, in a tent beside her husband's claim, Louisa was delivered of a son on June 16, 1867, with a neighbor's wife acting as midwife. The child was christened Henry Archibald Lawson. The "Archibald" was a mistake—the parents had intended to call the boy "Herzberg" after his father, but the parson misheard, and his error was accepted. "Lawson" was the Anglicized form of his name which Peter Larsen had adopted.

He had little luck in his gold search. Soon he was back at Eurunderee, then off to a new strike at Gulgong, but too late for much chance of success. Mining had proved for him a hopeless way of supporting a family, and Peter decided, or was persuaded, to return to Eurunderee, now derelict as a gold field, and to take up land to farm. Australian land laws of the time made it possible to acquire a smallholding at a nominal price.

The district was not good agricultural or grazing country. What rich land there was had already been pre-empted. Peter, afflicted with the incurable disease of gold fever, had hopes of rediscovering the lost seam, and therefore selected his land near to its line, disregarding the unsuitability of the land for farming. Henry Lawson later wrote of the selection:

> Our selection, about three hundred acres, lay round a little rocky, stony, scrubby, useless ridge, fronting the main road; the soil of the narrow sidings, that were not too steep for the plough, was grey and poor, and the gullies were full of clay from the diggers' holes. It was hopeless—only a lifetime of incessant bullocking might have made a farm of the place.[1]

Frank Dalby Davison, novelist and farmer, has corroborated that verdict.

Circumstances were no more kindly than the land. Drought hung over the district:

> Blazing heat that made Granite Ridge and The Peak seem molten masses turned out on the scrub. Blue-grey ragged bush and the ashes of a soil. We drove the few cows to the creek twice a day, through private property, and there was always trouble about alleged loitering and the sliprails. The cows would lay [*sic*] in the shade for the rest of the day, and lived on the water, some wheaten chaff we had collected and the native apple-tree boughs we had lopped down in "the cool of the evening." Then—on the strength of the straw and the wheaten chaff, I suppose—I was sent some miles to bring a wall-eyed steer and a barren heifer that were going as a gift to whoever would come and fetch them. And they brought "the ploorer" amongst our cows. Then I used to bleed them by cutting their tails and ears in the sickening heat, and was often sick over the job.[2]

When drought broke, and the pleuro-pneumonia passed, there was rust in the wheat, followed by smut. The farm never supported the Lawsons even at subsistence level. At times their diet was restricted to bread, treacle, and dripping. Peter, who had a sailor's neat and adaptable hands, took jobs as a contracting carpenter. Often he must travel six miles to a job, put in a twelve-hour day, and journey back to do what he could about the farm in the evening.

Louisa helped by doing home-tailoring contract work—a notoriously sweated trade—and by organizing deals in cattle. The obtaining of that barren heifer, to which Henry bitterly refers, was no doubt one of Louisa's strokes of initiative. She also did much of the work round the farm, more to her taste than the boredom of domestic chores which she tended to neglect or to leave to Henry. His younger sister Gertrude has written, "Henry carefully fanned the flickering flame of my puny existence and it is only due to his care that I am writing this story to-day." [3]

In those premechanized days, without benefit of phosphates, the life of the Australian smallholder on poor land was a driven monotony of back-breaking toil, which was too often heartbreaking as well. It would be more depressing still in the surroundings of a dying gold field. Heaven knows how that pocked and withered landscape looked to Peter Larsen, who had spent his early years in the lovely seaside town of Arandaal.

I *"The Child in the Dark"*

The selector's weight of dreariness inevitably falls heaviest on his children, who must be pressed into service almost as soon as they can walk—and most heavily of all on the eldest son. Lawson once wrote some verses on the theme of the prodigal son—a new interpretation with the elder son seen as the focus of sympathy. He writes:

> The elder son on barren soil,
> Where life is crude and lands are new,
> Must share the father's hardest toil,
> And see the father's troubles through.
> With no child-thoughts to match his own,
> No game to play, no race to run;
> The youth his father might have known
> Is seldom for the elder son.[4]

This loneliness was not helped when a catarrhal attack in Lawson's ninth year affected his hearing. By fourteen, he was severely deaf, an affliction which remained with him for life.

Until after Lawson's eighth birthday, there was no school at Eurunderee. When it came, it was naturally a pretty rough-and-ready institution. Henry was a biddable child—something of a youthful prig, it would seem. In later years, he was shown the Punishment Book of the old school, and ruefully commented that his name did not appear in it, adding, "It comforts me to think that I've/Made up for it since then." [5]

He regarded this early blamelessness as evidence that he lacked boyish spirit, and other evidence supports that view. Certainly he was, in modern educational jargon, an "isolate," shrinking from contact with other children. He became worse when the Lawsons quarreled with the schoolteacher, and he and his brother were sent for a while to a Catholic school in a neighboring town, where the sensitive, countrified, deaf "Proddy" was easy meat for the ingenious savagery of schoolboy teasing. He developed at this time a dislike of fighting of almost pathological intensity, which stayed with him. He did not lack physical courage, and he could fight with a clumsy tenacity when he was moved thereto by a sense of a righteous cause; but the idea of violence disturbed and revolted him. One of the most intensely felt passages he ever wrote describes this feeling in a man forced into fisticuffs. Other evidence suggests that the incident is based on an experience of Lawson's, with only minor changes of circumstance.[6]

Tough and lonely as Lawson's childish conditions were, there was nothing inevitably destructive about them. Indeed, in terms of the log-cabin-to-White-House kind of legend, they would be seen as a valuable schooling in moral strength. If in fact the conditions of Lawson's childhood destroyed him as a man—and perhaps helped to make him as a writer—it was not because he was a too early and a too hopeless slave of the cows, or because his deafness shut him off from his fellows; the explanation lies in deeper and less survivable influences.

When Louisa Albury at eighteen married the unromantic little foreigner of thirty-three, she was not in love with him. Her circumstances at the time were frustrating. Her father was a Kentish-born peasant who could not read or write, but he was very much a personality. Cranky, opinionated, loud-voiced and immensely vigorous, he was a "character" who provided some wonderful copy for his story-writing grandson.[7] He had married, after his migration to Australia, an English-born girl, Harriet Winn, who had some education and transmitted to her children a love of reading. Louisa inherited a good deal of her father's vigor, determination, and impatience. Her temperament is suggested by a story she told of herself, apparently with pride. She is describing an encounter with a man who had come to her office in Sydney—after her escape from marriage—to borrow a printing block, and had "turned nasty" when it was refused:

> I asked him three times to go and he wouldn't, so I took up a watering-pot full of water that we had for sweeping the floor, and I let him have it. It went up with a s-swish and you should just have seen him! He was so nicely dressed—all flannel and straw-hat, and spring-flowers in his button-hole; and it wet him through—knocked his hat off and filled his coat-pockets full of water. He was brave, I'll say that; he wouldn't go; he just wiped himself and stood there getting nastier and nastier, and I lost patience. "Look here," I said, "do you know what we do to tramps in the bush that come bothering us? We give 'em clean water first, and then, if they won't go we give 'em something like this." And I took up the lye-bucket that was used for cleaning type; it was thick with an inch of black scum on it like jelly, that wobbled when you shook it. I held it under his nose and said, "Do you see this?" And he went in a hurry.[8]

Photographs of Louisa confirm the impression made by that story. They show a face of grim, juiceless strength—the kind of face you could break bricks against. Her driving nature early developed cultural ambitions: although these came from her mother's influence, they were not encouraged by Mrs. Albury. She was a quiet, womanly woman, a lower middle-class Cockney, driven to emigration as a domestic servant because she was at odds with her step-father. She found her daughter's rebellious ambitions presumptuous. Certainly Louisa's illiterate and domineering father would have had no sympathy with them. So there she was, working in a pub in a rough frontier community, wasting her fine singing voice on the miners, and solacing herself with the composition of verse. In this situation, Peter Larsen arrived with his proposal. Louisa later wrote, "I married to relieve Father of at least one of a large family. . . . Peter was almost a stranger to me when I accepted him." [9]

If she hoped for escape through marriage, she was woefully mistaken; she had slammed a dungeon door on her ambitions—and the official sentence read "Life, without remissions." Her daughter Gertrude says that the marriage was acknowledged a failure within two weeks of the wedding.[10] Childbirth in a tent beside a hole in the ground with no gold in it; the luckless traipsing to other gold fields; the desolate selection without a decent house on it; battle void of grounded hope; the dreary tyranny of domestic routine with four small children; the death of a baby; the felt capability for success within her, the compulsive thirst for it, joined to the realization that her husband had the habit of failure; the neighbor's friendly response to his quiet warmth, and their affronted recognition of her contempt for their cultureless stagnation—these explain much in that face in the photographs. It is not a face that invites compassion, it never could have been even in Louisa's girlhood; but only the unimaginative could withhold sympathy.

Louisa found such outlets as she could in the writing of verses, which the local papers published, and in bitter quarrels with her husband—Peter was a pleasant, gentle person, but he had a quick temper. Outside their room lay the hypersensitive lonely child whose deafness could not shut out those raised voices. In many respects the menage had a strong resemblance to that of the family of D. H. Lawrence; but there is a large, a decisive difference. Louisa did not shower on her son the intense possessive love which Mrs. Lawrence bestowed on David. If she ever had any power of love, it had been parched out of her by the droughts of her life. She seems to have had little to give to the son begotten in that disillusioned second month of her marriage, when the teen-aged girl who had devoured the novels knew what lay beyond the wedding bells of their happy endings.

In the fragment of autobiography which Lawson wrote, he says little of his relationships with his mother. He writes early in it: "I don't want to write a bitter line if I can help it, except it be against my later self." [11] He could not keep to that resolution; but he does at least soften the picture by evasion. He has much to say of his father; and Jim Gordon, a close friend of Lawson, in a piece of verse in which he describes Henry reminiscing in 1917, writes: "'My father's heart was gold,' he said,/For Lawson loved his sire." [12] But Gordon is discreetly silent about Mrs. Lawson, which is in itself a revealing omission, for both Lawson and Gordon were sentimental fellows with simply conventional moral valuations, who would be eager to acknowledge debts to a mother. In the Autobiography, Lawson writes of his father:

I don't believe that a kinder man in trouble or a gentler nurse in sickness ever breathed. I've known him to work hard all day and then sit up all night by a neighbour's sick child.[13]

and there are many other affectionate tributes to Peter. There are none to Louisa. Peter is described as "Father," but Louisa as "the mother." That chilling particle is dropped once, when Lawson is describing the death of her baby.[14]

He makes an admission, necessary to the picture he has to convey, of part of the truth: "Home life, I might as well say, was miserably unhappy, but it was fate—there was no-one to blame." [15] Later, candor seems to be forced out of him against a wavering intention to maintain his suppression of bitterness:

And then the craving for love, affection, even consideration from a quarter where there was none: the sympathy, love, even worship, wasted in a quarter where there was none.[16]

That quarter could only have been Henry's mother. Indeed Henry's Aunt Emma, with (and on) whom he lived for much of his life, declared "I think I was the only mother he ever knew." [17]

Lawson gives us a fuller and more aggressively accusatory picture in his story "The Child in the Dark." [18] This is nominally fiction; but detail after detail in it accurately mirrors the life of the Lawson family as we know it from other sources, and there is no touch which conflicts with such sources. There is a strong presumption that it is a direct transcription from life. It concerns a boy—of ten or thereabouts—overloaded with chores, oversensitive, emotionally overcharged; his father deprived of happiness, but gently affectionate toward his son; the boy's mother, a self-centered scold who uses a sick headache as an excuse for a slatternly neglect of her children and housework. The youngster has struggled to complete her tasks as well as his own, until he is overtaken by illness. His father tends him as well as he can. The wife screams from her bed, "For God's sake, Nils, take that boy into the kitchen or somewhere, or I'll go mad. It's enough to kill a horse." That detail may be a fictional dramatization of the situation; but it expresses Lawson's belief that Louisa had no love for him, as well as his lifelong conviction that he had thereby been deprived of a basic human need.

II *Struggle in Sydney*

In 1883, Peter and Louisa separated by mutual consent. The wife, taking the younger children with her, soon made tracks for the cultural opportunities of Sydney. For a while, Henry worked with his father on building contracts; it might have been a happier time, but the physical conditions were grim and Peter was growing morose. Soon Louisa called for her son's presence in Sydney; the family needed him as a bread-winner, since her tailoring work brought in little. He was then fifteen years old.

Henry found work as a painter, a trade in which he had gained some experience while he was working with his father. The carriage-works where he was employed was a long rail trip from his home, and he must rise very early; from departure to return was a thirteen-hour day. The tough youngsters from the city slums with whom he worked thought the hypersensitive kid from the country "a bit ratty"; he had no way of meeting their kind of crude badinage, although it was basically good-natured. Lawson has left some record of these days in his Arvie Aspinall stories.[19] At the time he wrote them, Lawson was strongly under the influence of Dickens, and these stories have a tone of sentimentalized Dickensian pathos; but the similarity to the work of the master may be due as much to the similarity of the two men's boyhood experiences as to the influence of the writer whom Lawson admired above all others.

He had hopes of escaping into some intellectual occupation. He attended night school with the idea of entering the university, but the cards were stacked against him. Lawson was not the scholar type; all his life, figures eluded his control. Deafness made class instruction difficult for him to follow. His health at the time was poor; accounts suggest that he may have had untreated adenoids. The family income did not run to the heaped-up plates which a fifteen-year-old needs. Before he reached his night classes, he had done a long day's manual labor. Unsurprisingly, he twice failed the Civil Service Entrance Examination, passing only in composition and history. That way of escape seemed blocked. It cannot have been easy news to break to an impatient and ambitious mother.

Meanwhile Louisa had been making her way. She became a known figure in the radical social movements of the time, particularly the feminist cause. The heat of battle suited her temperament, and the male sex was an enemy which she could attack with relish. She somehow managed to buy a propagandist sheet called *The Republican;* overcoming even greater difficulties, she started up a feminist paper which she called *Dawn*—the first of its kind in Australia—and continued to produce it until 1905. By that time Australian women had gained the right to vote, and Louisa could claim some of the credit for a victory won nearly twenty years before English women, or New England women, were enfranchised. She had come a long way from the serfdom of the selection.

III *The Beginning Writer*

It is uncertain how Lawson came to try his hand at writing; his own accounts are vague and confused. He had had some literary ambitions as a child, which Louisa encouraged. No doubt the general emphasis on journalistic work in the home turned his thoughts in that direction. According to Gertrude Lawson, Louisa was more directly influential. Henry was at once highly emotional and strongly idealistic. When a radical agitation which he supported was defeated he was overwhelmed with depression. "There's nothing I can do about it," he moaned. "Yes, there is. Write, my son," Louisa responded, and roused her despairing son from his hopelessness.[20]

The first clear emergence of Lawson as a writer took place on October 1, 1887, when he "made" *The Bulletin* for the first time—the prime aim, at that time, of all right-thinking young Australians with literary ambitions. His contribution, "The Song of the Republic," was a lively (and conventional) expression, in ballad form, of that combination of nationalistic and radical sentiment which was the dominant Australian ideology of the epoch. Lawson has recorded the excitement which his first appearance in important print brought to him,[21] and well it might. He had passed his twentieth birthday and was experiencing the taste of success perhaps for the first time in his life.

At the same time he was learning to appreciate another taste. When he received his first check from *The Bulletin,*—for £1–7–0—he was working on a country job with a congenial group of young fellows (people almost always liked Lawson when they got close enough to him to pierce his melancholy and his sense of social incompetence, and to recognize the strength of his sincerity, and the warmth, generosity, and gentleness of his nature). With these cronies he discovered a liking for beer, consumed in quantities which his low capacity could not handle. There seems no limit to the malicious ingenuity of Lawson's bad fairy. Having contrived for him the childhood conditions which predisposed him to alcoholism, she gave the screw another twist, and endowed him with a poor head for liquor.

Through the mouth of Joe Wilson—a character largely based on self-portraiture—Lawson has said:

> "I only drank because I felt less sensitive, and the world seemed a lot saner and better and kinder when I had a few drinks: I loved my fellow-man then, and felt nearer to him. It's better to be thought wild, than to be considered eccentric or ratty." [22]

Psychologists no doubt have a longer word for it, but perhaps get no nearer to the truth. Another Joe Wilson remark carries the diagnosis a stage deeper:

> "I wasn't a healthy-minded average boy: I reckon I was born for a poet by mistake, and grew up to be a bushman and didn't know what was the matter with me—or the world." [23]

For "poet," as the popular cultural mythology of the time understood that term, read "one nakedly sensitive, swift and deep in emotional reaction."

On his return to Sydney, Lawson became more active as a writer, although he earned little by it. To the attempts at popular balladry, which he had at first essayed, he added the writing of short stories—and on these his literary reputation today mainly rests. They were as original as his verse was conventional. His popular reputation with Australian readers was established with unusual speed: he was regarded, not only with admiration, but with an affection not often displayed toward writers. He seemed to express popular Australian sentiment with a satisfying accuracy, to be identified with his readers with a rare wholeness. That view had some elements of truth, but it also failed to perceive the highly individual and subjective attitude to life which underlay the simplicity of form and of ethical content in Lawson's work.

In these years of growing repute, Lawson was also establishing himself as a personality in the radical movement of the time. It will be convenient to discuss his political outlook in another chapter. Here, it will be sufficient to say that Labour Party enthusiasts of his day welcomed him partly for his personal quality and because his generosity of compassion fitted with their idealisms, partly because the polemical ballads which he wrote influenced a popular audience, inciting a combative radical response. At the same time, Labour Party men regarded him a little patronizingly, for he clearly lacked political sense and practicality—practicality in the urban, sedentary application of the term, for Lawson had a good pair of hands. He could best counter his sense of insecurity when he was exercising his skill as a bush carpenter, or instructing some uneducated townsman in the art of rolling a swag.

Lawson's political contribution was not limited to ballad writing. He also turned out more direct prose propaganda for various papers professing a Labour Party ideology. Most of this work was unpaid, for Lawson disliked taking money for his services to the cause.

He had also found a place in the Bohemian circle of Sydney journalists and writers. He was a little distanced from them by his melancholy, his deafness, and by a rankling sensitivity over his failure to acquire advanced education; but their hedonistic good fellowship suited the sense of comradeship which was the strongest element in Lawson's ethical creed. Perhaps the outlook of this group had serious disadvantages for a man struggling against a growing addiction to beer, as a remark of Lawson's suggests. During a stay in the New Zealand city of Auckland, he was without work and was reduced to sleeping in a pipe destined to form part of a new reticulation system. An old friend rescued him, gave him houseroom, and asked why he had not obtained help before. "There are any number of fellows, Tom," Lawson replied, "who'll ask a fellow to come and have a drink, but not one in a thousand thinks of offering me a feed." [24]

If economic security still eluded him, he acquired, during this period, the dignity of book publication. His first volume was a slim collection of verse and stories privately printed in 1894 on Louisa's press, and under the pressure of her energies. It was an amateurish piece of book production, and it had scarcely any sales. Two years later, Angus and Robertson decided to publish two volumes of bush ballads, by "Banjo" Paterson and Lawson, respectively. Paterson's volume was a dazzling success; its sales soon reached the 100,000 mark. Lawson's book, *In the Days When the World was Wide,* could not rival this, but rapidly achieved the healthy figure of 8,000-odd sales. It was followed in 1896 by *While the Billy Boils,* a volume of short stories which also did well.

IV *Brisbane and the Bush*

During the nineties, Lawson's life in Sydney was interrupted by a series of forays to other surroundings. His psychological insecurity made him restless, always wishfully believing that a settled place in life for him lay over the horizon. Of the six journeys which he made during this decade, two have a special importance for his work.

In 1890, Lawson accepted a job on the journalistic staff of *The Boomerang,* a radical weekly published in Brisbane: his salary was £2 a week, a fairly good wage for a skilled workman at that time. This job brought Lawson into contact with a group of impressive minds; the twenty-two-year-old who had mainly known the derelict gold field and the painter's workshops must have been badly in need of such broadening influences. The personal force behind *The Boomerang* was William Lane, a Socialist leader of limited administrative ability, but of passion and energy, qualities which spilled out in a fiery oratory. His outlook had the kind of glowing Utopianism which appealed strongly to Lawson. Lane, although still closely connected with *The Boomerang,* had passed over the editorship to Gresley Lukin, a member of a well-known Queensland family of professional-class status. Lukin had also gathered in a highly promising literary journalist in his early twenties, A. G. Stephens, who was to be associated with Lawson during most of the latter's career. Stephens's ability soon caught the eye of Archibald, and he became the literary editor of *The Bulletin.* He shared Archibald's ambition to create a vigorous school of Australian writing, and his knowhow effectively implemented that aim.

On *The Boomerang,* Lawson's main routine task was the preparation of the Country News column. He conceived the idea of turning its items into rhymed jingles printed as prose; he must have been one of the first exponents of this journalistic gimmick.

The staff of the paper became accustomed to the steady thump of Lawson's boots as he tramped about the office muttering over possible rhymes. He thus learned a truth which was to stand him in bad stead throughout his career, that "you can rhyme anything if you stare at it long enough between whiles of walking up and down and scratching your head." [25] Lawson thoroughly enjoyed his period on *The Boomerang,* and it was a bitter blow for him when an economic depression forced its proprietors to cease publication.

A little later, Lawson, still broke after the collapse of his job, asked Archibald to stake him on a trip to Bourke in a search for copy which might prove of ultimate benefit to *The Bulletin.* Archibald gave him a railway ticket and £5 in cash. Bourke was a railhead town which served the expansive cattle and sheep country of northern New South Wales and southern Queensland. It was also a center of militant union activity among the pastoral workers, and Lawson was warmly received by the Labour enthusiasts in the town. Bourke was very much a frontier settlement, a dreariness of iron-roofed shacks set in the featureless arid plain, and it was even browner and barer than usual in the drought year in which Lawson struck it. It was also appallingly hot. Lawson has recorded the standing joke about the Bourke man who died and went to Hell—he sent back for his overcoat.

The people were rough, thirsty, boisterous, and given to gory fist-fights activated by a lack of other congenial forms of entertainment rather than by any animosity of spirit. They were a vigorous and warm-hearted folk, staunch practitioners of that religion of Mateship of which Lawson was an adherent. In later life he wrote nostalgic verses about Bourke, with a warmth of affection which he could never feel for the Eurunderee where he had spent his boyhood:

> No sign that green grass ever grew in scrubs that
> blazed beneath the sun;
> The streets were dust in Ninety-two, and hard as bricks
> in Ninety-one.
> On glaring iron roofs of Bourke the scorching, blinding
> sandstorms blew,
> No hint of beauty lingered there in Ninety-one and
> Ninety-two

Save grit and pulse of generous hearts—great hearts
 that broke and healed again—
The hottest drought that ever blazed could never parch
 the souls of men;
And they were men in spite of all, and they were straight,
 and they were true;
The hat went round at trouble's call in Ninety-one and
 Ninety-two.[26]

(At this point it seems advisable to digress—or to anticipate—and to make clear a point to which we shall have to return. A reader unfamiliar with Lawson, encountering such a passage as this, is likely to wriggle uncomfortably and to wonder why a book should be devoted to the study of the contriver of such verse as this. Lawson's balladry usually produces some such effect on those with developed literary tastes. The remarkable point about him is that the same reader, encountering a Lawson story presenting identical feelings about the men of Bourke, is likely to find it masterly.)

In Bourke, Lawson formed a friendship with Jim Gordon, who was something of a balladist (under the pen name of Jim Grahame). Gordon wanted to seek a shearing job in the country "back o' Bourke," and Lawson decided to go with him. Some idea of the scale and solitude of the country is conveyed by the fact that the sheep station for which they were bound occupied 1,000,000 acres. Lawson was able to pick up a job in the shearing shed. When the wool was "cut out," he and Gordon made off for Queensland (on foot) and wandered about the wool country, signing on for jobs when they could and scrounging their tucker when they could not. By the middle of 1892, Lawson had had enough of bush hardship, and made for Sydney as a kind of supercargo, nominally in charge of sheep being trucked down to the city.

Archibald's £5 investment brought him rich returns. Lawson had found the kind of copy which precisely suited his talents and his temperament. Throughout the rest of his career he was using the material which his steady and precise gift for observation had garnered during his eighteen months in that harsh country. More than half of Lawson's fiction can be traced to one of two sources: anecdotes about Eurunderee neighbors which were current in the

Lawson household, or the experiences he encountered, and the yarns he heard, on that trip to Bourke and the "back of beyond."

V *Marriage: New Zealand Asylum*

Late in 1895, Lawson met a girl called Bertha Bredt, step-daughter of a bookseller at whose shop the radical enthusiasts were accustomed to foregather. Henry fell in love with a swiftness characteristic of his impulsive nature. Within a week he began proposing to her; but he had to keep it up for nearly six months before he got "yes" for an answer. Even then stratagem was necessary to break down Bertha's delaying tactics and bring her to the altar on April 15, 1896. The delays do not indicate that Bertha failed to return Henry's love, merely that she retained a measure of prudence. Her family strongly opposed the marriage, as did most of the couple's friends. They realized that Lawson's inability to stay sober or to earn money made him a poor matrimonial prospect. According to Bertha's account,[27] it was a happy marriage apart from the difficulties created by Henry's drinking.

About a year after the marriage the couple left Sydney for New Zealand. They had no money, but they were armed with a letter of introduction to the New Zealand Premier who had recently formed the first Labour Party government to take office anywhere in the world. A member of the cabinet who knew Henry was instructed to consider the possibilities, and he succeeded in meeting the conditions which Bertha asked for—the provision of a job somewhere miles from a pub, and where she could do most of the work. He arranged with the Minister of Education that a Maori school at Mangamaunu—a remote settlement unprovided with the dangerous amenities of civilization—should be reopened, and that Henry and Bertha should be appointed head and assistant teacher, respectively.

According to Bertha, the couple here achieved something like idyllic relations; but her account should probably be regarded skeptically. The fashion for intimate candor had not yet been established; a measure of discreet suppression is to be expected in the circumstances. Moreover, there were reservations in Henry's mind of which she was probably aware only through the moodiness which they inspired. From Mangamaunu, Lawson wrote to an old friend:

So the days of my riding are over,
  The days of my tramping are done—
I'm about as content as a rover
  Will ever be under the sun;
I write, after reading your letter—
  My mind with old memories rife—
And I feel in a mood that had better
  Not meet the true eyes of the wife.

You must never admit a suggestion
  That old things are good to recall;
You must never consider the question:
  "Was I happier then after all?"
You must banish the old hope and sorrow
  That made the sad pleasures of life:
You must live for Today and Tomorrow
  If you want to be just to the wife.

. . . .

No doubt you are dreaming as I did
  And going the careless old pace,
But my future grows dull and decided,
  And the world narrows down to the Place.
Let it be. If my reason's resented,
  You may do worse, old man, in your life;
Let me dream, too, that I am contented—
  For the sake of a true little wife.[28]

But if Bertha's picture is tinted with rose-madder, there is no reason to doubt that things were going pretty well for the Lawsons during the early months of the Mangamaunu stay. Henry managed to sneak off sometimes to the nearest settlement that had a pub; but his life was generally sober—indeed, he may have had less need to drink while he was living in isolation, with no call to drug his unsociable inhibitions. Moreover, for the first time, he commanded conditions for his writing which suited him. Such accounts as exist suggest that Lawson liked to write slowly, shaping his stories and refining their detail with a stubborn ruminative thoroughness. Hitherto he had had to work under conditions better adapted to journalistic improvisation than to evolved literary creation. In the Maori school he had leisure and solitude. He shared the teaching work with Bertha, but this left him with plenty of space in his days.[29]

VI *Return to Sydney*

Useful though the isolation and financial security of the life at Mangamaunu was to Lawson, it is not to be expected that it would satisfy so restless a man for long, and his melancholic tendencies soon began to assert themselves. The retreat from Mangamaunu was not, however, due to Henry. The birth of Bertha's first child was approaching, and a home so far from medical help was undesirable. The Lawsons resigned their appointment in time for their son Jim to be born in the New Zealand city of Auckland. As soon as Bertha was fit to travel, the family sailed for Sydney.

After his months of isolation, Lawson found reunion with his Bohemian friends irresistible, with the result that too many of the too few sixpences he was earning went over the pub counters. Soon there was a bailiff in the home; characteristically Lawson made friends with him and took him off to the local, whence he walked out of the Lawsons' lives. Friendly admirers conspired to rescue him and wangled him a job in the Government Statistician's Office. It was a strange occupation to thrust upon a poet who could not handle figures confidently, but it was made clear to Lawson that he was not expected to work. Official government patronage of the arts scarcely existed in Australia at that time, but the good-natured Sydney hedonism could informally contrive it. Provided Lawson attended the office for the regulation hours, no questions would be asked and he could spend his time at his desk in literary composition. This well-intentioned scheme did not work. Lawson's restlessness could not accept incarceration in an office, and he persistently broke the one condition imposed on him. He was soon out of a job—and complaining of the hapless lot of a writer in a Philistine community. One may gauge how things were going by Lawson's next refuge—an inebriates' home. Bertha said the treatment did Henry a lot of good, but if this were so, it wore off as rapidly as such cures usually do.

VII *Economics of Authorship in Australia*

Soon the restlessness was reasserting itself; but this time Lawson had his sights set higher than usual—on London and an attempt to establish his reputation in a wider field, where the financial rewards of success would be greater. Lawson was convinced, as were many of his associates, that Australia treated her writers ungratefully. In 1899 he wrote an article for *The Bulletin*, called "Pursuing Literature in Australia," which concluded:

> My advice to any young Australian writer whose talents have been recognised would be to go steerage, stow away, swim, and seek London, Yankieland or Timbuctoo—rather than stay in Australia till his genius turns to gall, or beer. Or failing this—and still in the interests of human nature and literature—to study elementary anatomy, especially as applied to the cranium, and then shoot himself carefully with the aid of a looking-glass.[30]

His view provoked strong dissent—notably from A. G. Stephens who answered Lawson effectively—but it nevertheless expresses a strong current of opinion among the Australian writers of the time. Since the view that Lawson was badly treated by his countrymen has often been repeated, and has been used as a stick with which to castigate the philistinism of Australians, it may be worth examining the strength of its basis with some attention. It was certainly true that Australian writers of Lawson's generation faced one serious difficulty: their possible audience was too small. In 1900 the population of Australia fell short of four million. Given nineteenth- or twentieth-century conditions of book publication and distribution, and of payment of authors, this is hardly enough to give a writer much chance of earning a good living. It was the limitation of the size of his audience, rather than its allegedly exceptional philistinism, which condemned the Australian writer to unbuttered bread.

Indeed, the figures of Lawson's sales suggest that the Australians of his time were by no means unresponsive to literature, provided it was a kind which suited their unsophisticated tastes. During his lifetime, nearly 300,000 copies of his books were sold within Australia, and his output was by no means large. Not many English writers of that time could boast sales of three million, the equivalent figure on a per capita basis (without allowing for the Englishman's easier access to overseas markets). Lawson's financial return need not have been meager. His first two books—ignoring Louisa's attempt to publish him without the support of a competent press or a selling organization—appeared in 1896. By 1900, 49,000 copies had been issued, and the demand for them was still steady. In that year two new volumes were published and were selling at the rate of 5,000 each a year. A. G. Stephens states that the standard rate of royalty for books of the kind was about ninepence a copy after the first thousand, which would have brought in over £2,000. Moreover, all the material in these books, and the later ones issued by Lawson, had already appeared in periodicals, together with much else which Lawson did not choose to reprint. The greater part of it had been accepted by *The Bulletin* which paid well for stories, badly for verse. Lawson did not produce prolifically, and perhaps his limited markets were soon saturated; but the return from this source must have been more than £350. Thus in his first five years as a book author, Lawson could have made an average income of about £450 per annum. It was not affluence, but it was at that time amply sufficient to maintain a family at a middle-class standard of comfort.

In point of fact, Lawson had received nothing like this sum, because he committed the author's business sin of selling his copyrights. This was not because wily publishers took advantage of the innocence of a young writer. George Robertson, head of the house of Angus and Robertson, was a shrewd Scot, but he was no chiseler; Lawson, in his more querulously alcoholic moments, complained that his publishers did him down, but in soberer moods he admitted Robertson's generosity. Later in life, Lawson wrote a poem, published after his death, in honor of Robertson. It bears on its title page the words "as some slight acknowledgement of, and small return for, his splendid generosity during years of trouble." [31]

Robertson has recorded the facts of the publication of that first volume of verse in 1896:

> Both the Patterson and the Lawson agreements provided for the equal division of profits between author and publisher. But three months later . . . Lawson commuted his interest for . . . £54. . . . Afterwards when Snowy [Paterson's volume] had such a success, we wrote voluntarily to Lawson to say that we would cancel the straight-out sale and consider the £54 an advance of half-profits. But in a short time we were forced to buy him out again; he thought that a profit-sharing agreement entitled him to 2/6, 5/-, or £5 whenever he wanted them —which very often was several times in one day.[32]

Lawson's defense against a charge that he threw away his chance of financial security would probably have been that he was too hard up to hold out until the royalties began to roll in. It is a weak defense for a thirty-year-old with no children, and a trade, not to mention the publishers' advances and the driblet of journalistic earnings which could have tided him over bad times. No doubt, to expect this economic continence of Lawson is to demand more than a man of his weaknesses could be expected to attain; but to blame the unresponsiveness of the Australian audience or the wickedness of commercial exploiters for Lawson's financial straits is absurd, and an outrageous injustice to his good friends Archibald and Robertson.

It may be said that creative artists often show Lawson's kind of fecklessness, and that a wise community will nevertheless ensure to them conditions in which they may work securely and with dignity. It is a reasonable claim and one which is being increasingly recognized today by public authorities; but in 1900 no Anglo-Saxon community thus interpreted its responsibilities. The need for public support of the arts, to replace the vanishing aristocratic patron, had yet to be recognized. Blame the philistinism or myopia of the age, if you will, for the poverty of Lawson, but not a specifically Australian philistinism. Artists of Lawson's temperament were starving in garrets all over the allegedly civilized world.

VIII *London Venture*

Before he left New Zealand, Lawson had already determined to try his luck in London, and thereby increase his prestige and the range of his potential audience.[33] In 1899, he wrote to Earl Beauchamp, at that time Governor of New South Wales, explaining his difficulties in Australia, the importance to him of English experience, and declaring that "within two years I can win fame and fortune in London."[34] Beauchamp, he understood, was a rich man; Lawson's own friends were poor. Would Beauchamp help to establish one of those Australian writers in whom he had already demonstrated his interest?

Judging by the preface which he constributed to a memorial volume paying tribute to Lawson,[35] Beauchamp was a good-natured, easy fellow who carried his rank unobtrusively. He was an enthusiastic supporter of the writers of his temporarily adopted country, and greatly admired Lawson's work. He invited the writer to dinner and offered to pay the fare of the Lawsons to London and to assist them in making contacts in England. Lawson promptly accepted the offer, although Bertha was less enthusiastic when he brought home the news, for her second child (a daughter named after her mother) was then only a few weeks old, and Jim was subject to convulsions.

Beauchamp's generosity was supported by others. The departing fortune hunter was honored at a valedictory dinner at which A. G. Stephens did the oratorical honors to an impressive audience. When Lawson's steamer called at Melbourne, a letter awaited him with instructions that he should visit John Longstaff, an up-and-coming painter, to sit for a portrait commissioned by a group of admirers headed by Archibald, and donated to the Sydney National Gallery. Its truth to character is clouded because Lawson has imprisoned himself in a best suit with a collar of lofty respectability; but Longstaff has effectively rendered the eyes, on which practically everyone who has written of Lawson has commented—large brown eyes, intensely sensitive, wistful, and quite devoid of any calculation or aggressiveness, the eyes of a charming dog who has learned to be wary of kicks but has not been soured by his knowledge that kicks abound. All adult portraits of Lawson fall short of full revelation because he sported a bushy moustache in the manner of his day; a photograph of him as a child shows a wavering mouth with a downward twist at the corners. It is a pathetically vulnerable mouth.

The episode of the portrait illuminates the contrast which convinced Lawson that he was the victim of financial injustice. It must be a rare occurrence for a National Gallery to hang the portrait of a writer barely into his thirties and of no social eminence. It suggests the remarkable reputation which Lawson had so swiftly established with the Australian public; but the reputation buttered no parsnips. On the one hand his picture hung beside those of His Britannic Majesty King Edward VII and Her Majesty Queen Alexandria at Longstaff's one-man show; but its subject had suffered bailiffs in the home, and one of his most popular ballads bears the title "When Your Pants Begin to Go."[36] This contrast between his repute and his material condition was, in fact, largely due to his fecklessness; but men do not readily blame themselves for their misfortunes if they can find other scapegoats, particularly if they are alcoholics. As Lawson wrote "The man is bitter against the world who has only himself to blame." [37]

Lawson was received in England with some *réclame*. Edward Garnett, a litterateur of considerable influence, befriended him and wrote articles enthusiastically praising his work. The editor of *Blackwood's Magazine* had written to Lawson in Australia, asking him to submit stories. Since *Blackwood's* still had high literary prestige, this was a wonderful opportunity which a struggling young writer should have seized with both hands; Lawson did nothing about it.[38] Now contact was established, *Blackwood's* bought some of his stories and undertook to publish a volume of his work.[39]

Other periodicals and publishers began to show an interest in the Australian with his unaffected approach to short-story writing, and his unusual subject matter. Opportunity was opening to him, but Lawson could not seize it firmly. He was writing well below the standard of his best work. A large part of the attraction of his writing lies in the completeness of his identification with his subject matter. He did not speak on behalf of the Australian bushman; he spoke as a bushman. Writing in the grayness of London, he could not see his native color, and his ear lost its responsiveness to the Australian drawl. He did not know the English well enough to write effectively of the life by which he was presently surrounded, although he tried. It is a difficulty which has often devitalized the work of expatriate Australians.

There were other troubles. Henry established his family in a village whence he made forays on London publishers and editors. Pubs were sprinkled through the London streets almost as freely as they were in Sydney, and Lawson had no regular occupation to keep him out of them. Bertha had a complete breakdown and had to go to a hospital, perhaps a euphemism for "mental home." [40] After her discharge, the family moved to dreary London lodgings. Later Lawson wrote of "days in London like a nightmare." [41]

There may have been a special influence which was weighing on Bertha and Henry. Before he left Australia, he had fallen in love. Hannah Thornburn was a girl in her early twenties whom Lawson had met before his visit to New Zealand. Some time before his departure for London, an emotional relationship developed between them; it is impossible to say whether or not they were physical lovers. Indeed, very little is known about Hannah.

Those friends of Lawson who knew about her have mostly maintained a discreet silence; one—Bertram Stevens—has described her as

> . . . a rather delicate, plain girl, the daughter of a weaknatured man who drank and was often out of employment. She was romantic: a poet of any kind would appeal to her, and Lawson, *the* Australian poet, was regarded with something like worshipful admiration. She supplied the flattery and encouragement he did not get from his wife.[42]

It is clear from verses which he wrote that Henry's mind was very much on Hannah during his London stay, but it is not clear what his intentions were. Perhaps he saw his problem with self-understanding when he wrote:

> You love me, you say, and I think you do
>   But I know so many who don't,
> And how can I say I'll be true to you
>   When I know very well that I won't?
> I have journeyed long and my goal is far;
>   I love, but I cannot bide,
> For as sure as rises the morning star,
>   With the break of day I'll ride.[43]

IX *Return to Disaster*

Early in 1902, Lawson decided to return to Australia—or was it to Hannah? He and Bertha traveled on separate ships, but that may have been merely a matter of convenience. There is some evidence that they may not have been on good terms. Lawson has written a sketch about a drunken spree in Antwerp which befell one John Lawrence, a name which he often uses when he is writing about himself. He there says:

> It is only fair to Jack to say that he left England in trouble—not of his own nor England's bringing on—and was coming home to a lot more of it: and he made up his mind to blunt it in foreign ports; perhaps he was wise.
>
> Jack and his friends found themselves in a cool place in a basement where there were girls and beer. The women spoke English and Jack had heard enough English from women to last him for the rest of his life . . .[44]

Bertha's ship was delayed by engine trouble, and Henry rejoined her at Colombo. He came on board expansively drunk. Bertha has written that she could not forgive him;[45] it seems likely that there was more behind her stiffness than even so public a display of her husband's old trouble. As Henry crossed the Indian Ocean with this thin-lipped disapproval accompanying him, his mind must have been leaping forward to Hannah, who admired as well as loved him. When he reached port, he learned that she had died a few days earlier. The last frail chance of salvation had slipped from his grasp.

A frail chance, certainly. It is not even sure that Hannah and Henry intended to attempt a permanent relationship. If they had, there was only an outside chance that Hannah's companionship would have cured, or effectively mitigated, Henry's alcoholism, even if one accepts the probability that the source of Henry's trouble was his feeling that he had been denied love. This much, however, seems almost certain: once this crashing blow had fallen, there was no hope for him. Henceforth, whenever the drink called, Lawson had the excuses of the malice of his fate and of an impressively romantic sorrow which needed to be drowned. No one so far advanced in his disease as Henry already was could hope to fight back against so heavy a handicap.

X *Decline and Fall*

The rest of Lawson's story is little more than the drearily familiar case history of an alcoholic; perhaps the most miserable feature of a miserable story is the fact that drink took another twenty years to kill him. It had already virtually destroyed his talent, aided, no doubt, by the depressive influence of Hannah's death. I have written that, in the "Joe Wilson" volume published by *Blackwood's,* Lawson seemed on the edge of exciting developments; but in fact it was the last volume in which Lawson's talent really displayed itself. Henceforth he was capable of little more than self-imitation. He wrote perhaps half a dozen stories which stand on the level of the second-best work of his good years. There are, more frequently, stray gleams of his authentic quality. The keenness of his eye and the direct flow of his ideas into words never left him, and they will suddenly flash out of one of his later stories; but his admirers today probably rarely trouble to open the volumes containing them.

Lawson, of course, knew that he was struggling vainly to regain his artist's power: it must have been his sorrow's crown of sorrow. There is a painful, wishful-thinking story, again about "John Lawrence," a writer who staged a recovery:

John Lawrence's last story, published in a monthly magazine, was making something of a sensation, for in it he had gone back to his old style, and surprised many friends and enemies, who had thought and hoped that he was written out, and the style dead.[46]

Lawson's personal life was also disintegrating. For a few months after his return from England, his marriage continued rather stormily. Then Bertha demanded a separation; she says that she did so regretfully for the sake of the children. She had secured a job—it seems that the generous George Robertson had obtained it for her—and was thus protected from Henry's uncertain earning power. He fought hard against separation, the demand for which, he believed, came from Bertha's relatives. They, or she, were no doubt right in believing that his presence in the home could not be good for the children. For that matter, a wife may reasonably protect herself from the demands of an alcoholic husband. Nevertheless, there seems an element of cruelty in this turning loose of a man who more than ever needed feminine sympathy and the comfort which his deep affection for his children brought him.

He found refuge with Mrs. Biers, a middle-aged boarding-house keeper, with a weakness for tending stray cats and their human counterparts. Lawson had two claims on her hospitable heart. The forlornness of his condition appealed to her; and she had a love of books and immensely admired his writings. For the rest of his life, she was his housekeeper in a small, unappetizing cottage.

He cannot have been an easy stray cat to mother, for his drinking had grown steadier and deeper. He developed a technique for cadging small sums to keep the liquor flowing, a clownish and shameless exploitation of old friends and even of new admirers he might meet, and to whom he would offer his autograph on a piece of paper inscribed "I.O.U. 2/-." Sometimes he would appear to some old friend busy in his office, hold up three fingers, and silently disappear with the proffered threepence.[47] Often he drank with a ring of deadbeats in a vacant lot, sharing the crude spirits which brought drunkenness cheaply and swiftly, and contributing to the recriminations against the wives and women who had deserted the sinking ships or helped to drive them on the rocks. His later writing sometimes celebrates the tough loyalty of "sinful" women, contrasting it with the righteous cruelties practiced by the respectable.[48] The note of contrast in these stories is new; but Lawson had treated with sympathy the figure of the good-hearted prostitute long before the debacle of his marriage.[49]

He soon acquired some familiarity with the inside of jails. Most of these experiences were a matter of an overnight stay in cells on the charge of "drunk and disorderly." This did not happen often, for Lawson and the constables on beat duty had a mutual regard for each other. Usually the cop who found Lawson incapable would put him in a cab and send him home. On several occasions, however, he served longer sentences for the crime of failing to keep up his maintenance payments to his wife. Prison must have been a horrible form of punishment to a man so sensitive and restless, who had committed self-destructive follies, but who, if the record speaks truly, was incapable of a meanness, a cruelty, or a deliberated aggression.

These experiences had one result of some value. Lawson had in these years constituted himself the champion of the social rejects. In this capacity he attacked the callous retributiveness of the prison system of the time notably in the ballad "One-Hundred and-Three." [50] It is rougher than most of his ballads, for it was written in jail and smuggled out. The idiocy of the code denied a prisoner sanctioned access to paper, so that Lawson had to use such meager scraps as friendly inmates could steal for him. These were insufficient to permit him to practice his normal patient revision. Despite the resultant metrical jumpiness and an appalling sentimentality in the last line, "One-Hundred-and-Three" is one of Lawson's best ballads, with the sting of its angry compassion sharpened by the accuracy, and the direct rendering, of its factual knowledge.

Lawson was proud to believe that he spoke for the rejected and that they valued his expression of their feelings. He has written of his verses:

> I've read them pencilled with a scrawl
> In dens where souls are black as jet.

My lines upon a prison wall
Are showing through the whitewash yet.

It is likely that the lines thus celebrated came from "One-Hundred-and-Three." Indeed, even today, the unwary or oversympathetic nocturnal stroller, who allows himself to be buttonholed by a down-and-out in the garrulous stages of drink, may have great chunks of that poem throatily elocuted at him.

XI *Rural Respites*

Some attempts were made by Lawson's friends to rescue him. In 1909, Mrs. Biers sought help from some of the faithful to get him out of jail. A deputation waited on Bertha to find out if she would consent to his release if his arrears of maintenance were paid—the sum was trifling. She explained that she was not concerned about the money, and had resorted to the legal charge which put him in jail because he had been coming to her house and making a nuisance of himself. She would willingly assist in obtaining his release if he would promise to leave Sydney. Lawson was angry at the condition but eventually agreed to be shipped to Mallacoota, where E. J. Brady, an old friend, had a camp in beautiful bush country. Thomas Mutch, a staunch friend who later became a New South Wales cabinet minister, went with him. Lawson greatly enjoyed this sojourn in peaceful conditions with congenial company. To a visitor, he said: "You know . . . there is a pub on the other side that I could get to if I wanted to. But I wouldn't let Tom down. I'm playing the game as Tom planned." [51] It is said that he kept off the drink for two years after this break.

In 1916, Archibald and others sought the help of the New South Wales Premier, W. A. Holman. He was a man of intellectual and human quality, and one of the Labour Party enthusiasts of the nineties, when Lawson had been connected with the movement. He was ready to help, and a plan was organized. The government would pay him £2 a week and give him and Mrs. Biers rent-free occupation of a cottage on the recently established Yanco Irrigation Settlement. In return Lawson was to include, when he relevantly could, accounts of the irrigation work in any stories or journalism which he wrote there. Holman included this condition so that Lawson would not feel himself the object of charity.

The planners probably saw two advantages in the scheme. Lawson had for years preached the doctrine of irrigation as the cure for the Australian curse of drought, of which he had had such bitter experience in his youth. He would therefore be able to fulfill his propagandist duties with a clear artistic conscience. Moreover, Yanco was a prohibition area, as befitted its devotion to water. This second advantage did not work out quite as the planners had hoped. The town of Narrandera, not very far from Yanco, had a publican with literary tastes, who considered it his cultural duty to supply a poet's liquor on credit and to transport it the necessary dusty miles. He probably never got his money, but he had his reward in a pleasant little sketch which Lawson wrote about him.[52]

It seems likely, however, that Lawson was usually sober during his Yanco stay, for some of the stories which he wrote there come near to the quality of his early work; and those who met him were impressed by his improved appearance. He was not, however, very satisfied and he did not give satisfaction to officialdom. The irrigation commissioners did not have Holman's detached view toward informal patronage of the arts, when its expenses were met from their financial grant. The occasional references to irrigation which Lawson wrote seemed to them a poor return for the money, particularly as those references included unsympathetic allusions to the prohibition regime. (Perhaps Lawson had a point: an area dry enough to need irrigation is likely to be hot and dusty enough to need beer.) There was friction, and Lawson periodically dispatched resignations which Holman promptly tore up. During the Premier's absence in London, his deputy received one of these resignations, and Lawson left Yanco after an eighteen months' stay.

XII *Lawson's Personality*

There had, of course, been a marked deterioration in Lawson's personality as well as in his writing, during the years of his heavy drinking. He acquired a habit of self-pity, varied by moods of self-denunciation which were scarcely less embarrassing in their nakedness. At certain stages of alcoholic impregnation, he was likely to discover improbable grievances and to abuse even his more faithful friends, although he usually apologized handsomely when he sobered up. Despite these not easily tolerated faults, much of Lawson's personal attractiveness survived to the end. There was a certain innocence about him which he never lost. The tone is suggested in a trivial incident told by Arthur Price:

> Once we wandered into a restaurant. It looked alright outside but on closer inspection we were dubious. So Henry strolled into the kitchen, had a good look round, satisfied himself in a perfectly friendly way that all was well and we settled down to dinner.[53]

One can feel the same quality behind the contribution which he made to a brochure in which Tom Mutch solicited the votes of the electors. Lawson throws overboard the pomposities proper to political occasions and adopts a disarmingly simple approach:

> In the first place I would like to say I don't agree with his politics at all—not a politic of them. As a matter of fact I don't agree with anybody's politics. But he has carried his swag with me, and was and is the straightest mate I ever had; and I made him smoke a pipe—and once got two medium beers consecutively into him. It took me three years to do these things, and now I reckon I ought to have a say in his affairs.
>
> He had directly opposite ideas to mine as to how to bake a Johnnie Cake; and he had as much sense of direction as a hen—I reckoned!—and would flutter off as obstinately as a reptile in the opposite direction to that in which I of course *knew* we should go to reach our next night's camp. *And we got there without a row.* If that isn't a test of mateship, I don't know what is. . . . Tom Mutch is the Straightest Mate I or anyone else ever had; and if he says he's going to do a thing, he's going to do it all right.[54]

That unconventional document is so much in character that I have no doubt that its simplicity of approach was not calculated; at the same time there is a certain shrewdness, also characteristic, in the performance. Given the tone of the Australian community of the time, it was probably a more effective vote-catcher than anything the professionals could have contrived.

With this innocence went a warmth and generosity which came from as deep a level as the melancholy which often seemed to contradict such qualities. Not all those cadged threepences were spent on beer. Some were carefully hoarded in his hatband to be tossed to the children of his neighborhood, who were his allies and friends.

Tom Mutch's summing-up conveys him well:

Patronage he resented, flattery he disdained: he scorned insincerity and hypocrisy he despised. His track through life was made more stony by a quick impatience that sometimes developed into temper. Yet he was magnificently unselfish.[55]

E. J. Brady's view echoes Mutch's:

I found in him during life a great charity for his fellows and their faults, a love of truth, a hatred of lies, and an almost childlike innocence of body, soul and mind.[56]

On September 2, 1922, Henry Lawson's dead body was found in the back yard of his cottage. An unfinished manuscript lay upon his writing table. The New South Wales government afforded him a state funeral, and the people of Sydney turned out in force to salute his passing. A statue commemorating him was erected in the Sydney Domain. Such posthumous honors did not impress E. J. Brady, the friend and fellow writer who had drunk with Lawson in the days of their Bohemian youth, and who had helped to keep him on the water-wagon during the Mallacoota interlude. He could not patiently think of those prim respectables who subscribed for a statue to the dead genius, and who had shrunk fastidiously from the unsteady figure cadging his drink money about Sydney.

Twenty-five years later, a tourist was visiting a collective farm on the Russian steppes. He was presented to an elderly peasant as "a novelist from Australia." The old eyes lit up. "A writer from Australia? Then, of course, you will know Henry Lawson. Tell me about him. . . . Ah, what stories those are!" [57]

Henry Lawson, the defeated man, the drunkard, the lover and the prose-laureate of the simple and the warm of heart, would have been happy in that victory.

CHAPTER 3

The Folk Speaker

HENRY LAWSON was affectionately regarded as a national figure while he was still in his twenties. It was a remarkable achievement, even if one allows for the smallness of the nation, its immaturity and its preceding lack of literary figures worthy of regard. It was the more remarkable because of the apparent lack of solidity in Lawson's work, a rivulet of verse, sketches, and short stories of seemingly frail structure. The warmth, almost the excitement, of that response rests on the feeling of his contemporaries that his work expressed the informing spirit and the emerging self-confidence of the nation.

The basis from which that appeal rose was the kind of subject matter which Lawson chose to treat. Indeed, he and his Australian contemporaries, in their choice of human themes, achieved something of a revolution. It was not an influential revolution, since their work was scarcely known outside the country in which they wrote, but it indicated a change of approach which was to spread during the early years of the twentieth century, and theirs seems to have been the first national literature to have experienced that change. For the first time for centuries, Western writing had escaped from the limbo of a middle-class point of view.

That may appear to be altogether too large a claim. Such a revolution may seem to have been achieved at least a generation earlier in other Anglo-Saxon countries. I doubt if that is really true. There was, certainly, so proletarian a writer as Burns long before—but even he, under the influence of his lionization by fashionable Edinburgh, had tried to write like a bourgeois literary man, and had thereby almost destroyed his talent. There was certainly Mark Twain, but even he did not fully have the courage of his popular convictions, or, rather, had not always the higher courage to disregard his wife's gentilities. Who else was there? Many, no doubt, would claim Dickens, and it is true that he achieved important social emancipations for the novel; but they were emancipations of a different kind. His surest mastery is of characters drawn from the lower ranks of the middle class. When he deals with working-class figures, his touch becomes less sure, his sentiment often thickens into goo. It is the Boffins, the Pecksniffs, and the Dick Swivellers who permanently people our minds. Bill Sikes, Joe Gargery, and Smike flicker and fade from the memory. When he does fully succeed with lower-class characters, they are usually servants and are, therefore, essential parts of the middle-class landscape.

There are other names which might be cited, but on closer inspection they usually turn out to be writing from a middle-class point of view. Their interest in working-class character arises from their sense of the spicy flavor which such exotics give to the dish. Such writers conducted their middle-class audience on a Cook's Tour of the Lower Orders. Foreign travel is so broadening to the mind.

To put the point in another way, these writers usually reserve their "straight" parts—the characters which express basic human qualities—for representatives of the middle classes. The lower-class figures are cast as "character parts," with the emphasis on the interest of eccentricity and of "humors," and treated with a touch of caricature. The Australian writers of the nineties have a very different approach. They see their working-class figures as the fully natural human beings representative of the basic motives, seldom finding in them the marks of eccentricity. Indeed, they almost reverse the European approach. Upper-class characters enter their books to be satirized in comic poses or to provide the plot with some needed element of villainy. (Lawson shows this tendency less than his Australian contemporaries.) There is no Cook's Tour of the lower orders because these writers were not writing primarily for a middle-class audience. For that matter, they were not usually themselves members of the middle class. They wrote of the people, for the people, from the people.

A proviso is perhaps desirable here, in modification of this large claim. It may be that parallel forms of writing existed elsewhere, particularly in America, but have not survived within the purview of the ordinary reader. Perhaps Jack London—an admirer of Lawson's work, by the way[1]—may not be the sudden emergence, significant of a twentieth-century change in the cultural weather, which he seems to the uninformed. If so, the voice of such a nineteenth-century proletarian writing fails to be heard by the ordinary reader against the more assured tones of the American middle-class writers. Australians are aware of their early proletarians, because in the nineties there was virtually no other audible voice. The representatives of the middle class lacked either the cultural maturity or the acceptance by their social inferiors which was needed before they could become effective leaders. It is also true that the proletarians had developed a self-confidence of an unusual firmness.

The Australian common man warmed to Lawson because he spoke for, from, and of the people, well enough to justify their belief in such a theme and such an audience. He was thus proving a principle of the mythology. Moreover, he spoke mainly of bush-life and its values, which were such important elements in that mythology.

It is true that Lawson sometimes wrote of city life. There are, for example, the Arvie Aspinall stories in which he uses the experiences of his years as an apprentice in the Sydney coach-building shops, endowing Arvie with much of his own youthful temperament. It may be significant of a certain strain in Lawson that he gives this self-representative the distinction of an early death, in the worst tear-jerking nineteenth-century style. There is also a story, "Two Larrikins,"[2] a sketch in which a young rough gets his girl into trouble. At first, he suggests to her an abortion, but her ingenuous tactics break him down and lead him to accept with satisfaction a decision to marry her. It is a sentimental piece, antithetic to the modern taste for "tough" interpretations; but it is convincing. Every touch in the dialogue—at least in the boy's share of it—has an authentic flavor. It is clear from this story that Lawson knew his slum types well and could achieve a warmth of sympathy with them. There are a few other city stories in Lawson's earlier work and many from the days of his decline, when he had lost touch with bush-life. There are also some stories and ballads which are based on his New Zealand and English experience. The greater part of his work, however, and almost all the best of it, is concerned with bush-life.

I *Lawson's View of Bush-Life*

Lawson does not give us a conventionally romantic picture of the country's greater opportunities for freedom, or its tranquillizing influences on personality, as do some of the New England rural writers. Nor has his bush-fiction anything in common with that remarkable form of modern folklore, the "Western." That genre is ultimately based on certain actualities of American frontier life, but it hardly pretends to render that life with anything like truth. It is not necessary to the success of the medium that it should be like anything real; it is only necessary that it should be releasingly unlike the dissatisfying conditions from which its urban reader is seeking imaginative escape. Apart from the youngest or most naïve of them, these readers do not suppose that it is telling the truth any more than the "Whodunnit" enthusiast supposes that an English manor house is littered with corpses and sinister butlers.

The Australian fiction writers composed with the bushman as an essential element in his audience. If Archibald's "intelligent prospector" did not respond to the Australian writer, that writer had missed his main mark. For that audience an escapist, romantic view of frontier life would not do. Indeed Australian fiction has shown an obstinate preference for the use of naturalism as a literary technique. It was adopted there before it had become established as the standard fictional approach in England during the early years of the twentieth century, and it continued in general Australian practice well into the 1950's, after the novelists of the older countries had grown restive against the method's restriction of imaginative appeal. The dominance of this approach was not due to any conscious theorizing or acceptance of literary influences. It seems to have arisen almost instinctively from the Australian's pride in what he considered his superior realism, his pragmatic attitude, and his loyalty to the standard of the "dinkum" in human behavior. Lawson certainly fully accepted the method in his prose, using verse forms when he was moved by more romantic impulses.

He approached his stories with the attitude of a portrait painter who judges his success by the degree of authenticity with which he has communicated the character of his sitter. Indeed, he carried the attitude so far that, except for a brief period when he attempted a new approach which he soon abandoned, he made very little use of the supports of strong plotting or of picturesque coloration. His attitude toward such devices was probably much the same as the very Australian one expressed by his protégé Miles Franklin in the Preface to *My Brilliant Career:*

> There is no plot in this story, because there has been none in my life or in any other life under my notice. I am one of a class, the individuals of which have no time for plots in their life, but have all they can do to get their work done without indulging in such a luxury.

Such an approach does not encourage a romantic attitude toward the interpretation of frontier life.

There was, however, a form of such romanticizing expressed in the verse of the bush-balladists. One often encounters there the kind of rose-tinting which appears in "Banjo" Paterson's best-known ballad, "Clancy of the Overflow":

> And the bush had friends to meet him, and their
> kindly voices greet him
> In the murmur of the breezes and the river on its
> bars,
> And he sees the vision splendid of the sunlit plains
> extended
> And at night the wondrous glory of the everlasting
> stars.[3]

II *Duel of Balladists*

Lawson had no sympathy with this attitude; indeed, it led him to a four-round literary punch-up with Paterson in the pages of *The Bulletin.* Years later Paterson revealed that this argument had been a put-up job. Both men badly needed cash at the time. Lawson had suggested to Paterson that if each attacked the other, in verse, the result should suit *The Bulletin*'s taste for spicy pugnacity. They would probably be allowed to keep the argument going for weeks. Paterson agreed. So the two touched gloves, winked on the blind side of the spectators, and set to. They were good pros, determined to give the ringsiders their money's worth, and they did not pull their punches.

The motives of the contest, then, were commercial rather than ideological, but the difference of opinion which it expressed was real enough. It arose from a difference in the kind of experience which each man had known. Paterson was the son of a squatter. (The term "squatter" has not the same connotation in Australian use as in American, although the origin is similar. The word soon lost any suggestion of the illegal acquirement of land, and meant simply a pastoralist in a large way of business.) His family had not been very successful and had lost its original holding to the Banks. It had not, however, known real hardship, and could afford to buy young Paterson a good education. He practiced as a solicitor, but sedentary routine did not appeal to him and he turned to journalism and ballad writing. This suited him better, but he still felt himself to be an Adam expelled from the paradise of his free and enterprising childhood on the station. His ballads often express the kind of nostalgia for bush-life which I have quoted. At the time of the joust, Lawson was just back from his eighteen months in the drought-stricken country back of Bourke, whereas Paterson had been sitting in his city office sighing for the freedom of the bush, at space rates.

More lasting differences affected their attitudes. As Paterson later put the point:

> We were both looking for the same reef—but I had done my prospecting on horse-back with my meals cooked for me, while Lawson had done his prospecting on foot and had had to cook for himself.[4]

The contrast was rather more bitter, if Paterson had only known it. The squatter's son had probably had his pony when he was three, and, within a few years, the pick of the station hacks at his disposal, and his free choice of country for gallops. Lawson has recorded a particularly sore grudge against the conditions on the Eurunderee farm:

> I had an old cart-horse and a light pot-bellied mare, with a stunted colt and filly as reserves. I had a good seat and it was a district of riders, but I never had a horse you could call a horse to ride—it was misery right down to the old patched borrowed saddle.[5]

A further difference of circumstances between the two men is also important. Considering how strongly the bush affected Lawson's writing, he had spent strangely little of his life there. If we make the necessarily arbitrary assumption that he first became intelligently observant of the larger aspects of his environment when he was about eight, there were the six years until his departure for Sydney at fourteen, there were eighteen months of the Bourke trip, and there were two other periods of a few months—say, eight years in all. During this time he had experienced three serious droughts each lasting more than twelve months (Lawson certainly had a gift for unhappy experience; records kept since the beginning of White occupation of Australia show an average of one drought year in eight). Paterson's experience was likely to have been very different. In estimating the potential of human happiness in an Australian rural district, it is advisable to consult the Rainfall Reliability map. The areas where Paterson and Lawson respectively spent their youths are only about 150 miles apart, but the lines on that map take a veering curve between them, to the disadvantage of Eurunderee.

To a modern reader, Lawson seems to have very much the better of the argument between the two versifiers. Paterson spends much of his vigor on personal attacks. No doubt the spectators enjoyed these hefty swings, but they do not score points on the referee's card. Lawson keeps close to the point. Stylistically, too, he has a straighter left. His eye observes closely, and he packs the weight of concrete statement. Here is the picture of drought conditions which he sets against the myth of "the southern poets' . . . fancy-view" of the Bush:

> "Sunny plains!" Great Scott! those burning wastes
> of barren soil and sand
> With their everlasting fences stretching out across
> the land!
> Desolation where the crow is! Desert where the eagle
> flies,
> Paddocks where the luny bullock starts and stares
> with reddened eyes;
> Where, in clouds of dust enveloped, roasted bullock-
> drivers creep
> Slowly past the sun-dried shepherd dragged behind his
> crawling sheep.[6]

Paterson had an effective answer to this—that drought was, after all, only a passing condition; but he can make little effect with his point. His reply tastes like a sodawater chaser to a neat whiskey:

Yet, perchance, if you should journey down the very
track you went
In a month or two at furthest, you would wonder what
it meant.
Where the sunbaked earth was gasping like a creature
in its pain
You would find the grasses waving like a field of
summer grain,
And the miles of thirsty gutters, blocked with sand
and choked with mud,
You would find them mighty rivers with a turbid,
sweeping flood.[7]

Although the modern reader has little difficulty in finding Lawson's view the more convincing, he cannot be sure that the bushmen reading their *Bulletins* at the time generally took the same view. They were, after all, patriots of the bush, and Paterson appeared to be celebrating that patriotism. Yet one doubts if this would have been their attitude, and such evidence as there is strengthens these doubts. Three *Bulletin* readers decided that this was a free-for-all and joined the scrap. All supported Lawson. One of them was Edward Dyson, a Sydney writer who had knocked about the bush a good deal in his younger days (he made a second intervention in the argument, in which he declared the fight a draw, with each writer declaring part of the truth). The other two intervening versifiers appear, from internal evidence, to have been bushmen, unless they were journalists adopting that persona. Each had the same idea of replying to Paterson in the form of a parody of "Clancy," and each makes virtually the same point, that it is easy enough for Paterson to talk glibly about the romance of the bush when he is living comfortably in Sydney,

And he sees a vista splendid when the ballet is
extended
And at night he has his glory with the comic opera
stars

but the man who lives the bush life knows that it is not romantic:

If the Banjo's game to fill it, he is welcome to my billet.[8]

The bushmen who felt a patriotism for their life also prided themselves on their realism of outlook, and it was Lawson who had presented the realistic view. It was no part of the myth to believe that the bush-life was easy or gently attractive. The bushmen knew all about its toughness and it formed an important element in their pride. No doubt they loved the country, as people usually do love the environment which conditions their lives; but they also saw it as the ineluctable enemy whom it was their role to subdue. A central doctrine of their creed was the belief that they had proved themselves in the kind of tough struggle which the townsman's life evaded. Their belief was in the bush-folk rather than in the landscape.

III *Lawson's View of the Bushman*

Here Lawson was with them as heartily as, and perhaps more convincingly than, Paterson. In his stories almost always, and usually in his verse, Lawson is far more concerned with character than with passion or event or landscape. He writes mainly of the bushmen and he admires them intensely. He ratifies the myth's insistence on their superior simplicity, strength, and cleanliness of response to life. Part of my analysis of his attitude, it will be most convenient to treat later. Here let me illustrate its essential nature by reference to the story "A Hero in Dingo Scrubs."[9] It is concerned with Job Falconer, a young sheep farmer in a small way. His wife's first pregnancy shows signs of culmination a little earlier than expected, and Job rides off for the neighboring town to bring back his mother-in-law, who is to act as midwife—and to make sure that the doctor who is booked for the delivery is being kept reasonably sober, a task which Job has assigned to his younger brother. He has a gun with him (for reasons which are convincingly explained). He decides to take a shortcut through forested country. His horse is frightened and swerves, smashing Job's leg against a tree. He manages to fall clear and to throw aside his gun. As he lies helpless, several facts are present in his mind. He knows that, without some clue, no one is likely to think of his having taken that shortcut, and that it may be days before anyone finds him in his immobilized condition. He also knows that the horse will make his way back to the farm. The alarm thus given, experts in bushcraft will swiftly assemble and backtrack the fresh hoofprints to where he lies.

But there happens to be another experience in his mind. When he was a boy, his father's horse had thus appeared riderless at the homestead. As it happened, the father had been swiftly found, not seriously hurt. Job's mother, however, had been so alarmed by that ominous appearance of the horse without its rider that she never recovered from the shock. Back at Job's own house his young wife waits, with no experienced woman nearer than seven miles to help her through a premature confinement provoked by shock. So he somehow manages to crawl to his gun, then to a log against which he rests the barrel, and shoots the horse. Then he faints from pain. As the story develops, he is swiftly rescued and all is well.

A reader aware of a certain streak of naïveté in Lawson may think that the title of the story is an accidentally happy piece of clumsiness. The student of Lawson, who rapidly learns to respect his delicate sureness of touch, will have no doubt that the title is no accident. Lawson has deliberately juxtaposed the opposite emotional suggestions of the word "hero" and the prosaic, homespun place name. He is saying in effect: "These are the plainest of plain men, living in plain and unromantic places, but they are distinguished by an unpretentious heroism which springs from a strength and delicacy of feeling."

The point of the title's contrast is further emphasized in Lawson's physical description of Job:

> According to a theory of mine, Job, to fit the story, should have been tall, and dark, and stern, or gloomy and quick-tempered. But he wasn't. He was fairly tall, but he was fresh-complexioned and sandy (his skin was pink to scarlet in some weathers, with blotches of umber), and his eyes were pale-grey: his big forehead loomed babyishly, his arms were short, and his legs bowed to the saddle. Altogether he was an awkward unlovely bush-bird—on foot; in the saddle it was different. He hadn't even a temper.

Another detail of the story makes the point of the unheroic tone of Job's heroism more neatly. When he is found, he insists that he must not be taken home lest the seriousness of his injuries should have a bad effect on his wife. He says "Take me to Poisonous Jimmy's and tell Gertie I'm on the spree."

The dramatic quality of the incident on which the story is built

—even when modified by the prosaic, realistic touches which Lawson has taken care to provide—is unusual in Lawson's work. Normally, he prefers to keep to the ordinary with an almost puritanical strictness, showing his bushmen more humdrumly occupied, but the quality which he displays to us in Job Falconer is that of which we feel the others are capable. Thus, "Telling Mrs. Baker" [10] is concerned with two drovers who find themselves on an outback trip saddled with a boss who is in the grip of drink and barmaids. They struggle on, doing their best to protect him against his weaknesses, until he dies in the d.t's. Certain duties of loyalty still remain to be discharged. The boss's brother has already been summoned by telegraph; but the drovers arrange for a funeral, and then one of them fights the shanty-keeper who has entrapped the boss into indulgence of his fatal weaknesses. (In the literature of the bush mythology there is only one abiding villain—the shanty-keeper who sells evil spirits and employs flash barmaids from the city, the more surely to entice bushmen returning to semicivilization into "blueing their cheques" at the pub).

This routine of loyalty comes easily enough to the natures of the drovers. One last task remains which is a good deal harder for them—to return to the boss's wife and pitch her a tale of his peaceful parting, of the respect with which his funeral was followed by the local people who had grown attached to him, and of the affectionate messages to his wife and family which he uttered on his deathbed. (Luckily they think in time to go through his papers, and destroy the letters and photographs from other women which are contained therein.)

The nearer they approach to their destination, the less they like their job. When they arrive at Mrs. Baker's house, their discomfort is increased by two circumstances: their hostess relieves them of their hats, so that they have nothing to do with their hands, and there is present at the scene Mrs. Baker's sister, the nice city girl. One of the two, at least—the narrator of the story—falls in love with her at first sight "but she was far and away above me and the case was hopeless" (one observes, incidentally, that the usual assumption of the inferiority of a "townee" does not apply when the representative is feminine, pretty, and not urbanly la-di-da). The pair blunder through their task—there are some pleasant touches of humor here—but they do it effectively, all the more convincingly, perhaps, because they seem so unsophisticated. Again, as in "A Hero in Dingo Scrubs," we are aware of a certain delicacy of feeling in the makeup of the bushman.

The sister shows a tendency to ask awkward questions, so Andy tips her a wink. Afterward the girl follows them out and points out that it would be safer if she knew the truth which they have concealed from Mrs. Baker. So they tell her as much of it as can be told to a girl, without breaching the nineteenth-century bushman's code of chivalry. It is then that the city girl pronounces that eulogy of the bushmen which I have quoted on p. 12. But the myth places little value on words, so Lawson confirms the sincerity of her view by a more convincing action. She reaches up and kisses each of them "fair and square on the mouth"; then she waves a farewell and runs back to the house.

The unheroic scale of this story is more characteristic than the Dingo Scrubs episode of the way Lawson liked to frame his eulogies of bushman character. It may seem to be too trivial and sentimental an episode to sustain what is in fact quite a lengthy story. It is wise to read the story, however, before adopting that point of view. Any summary of a Lawson narration inevitably destroys the convincingness and the sense of significance with which his artistry can endow the frailest-seeming fictional structure and the most simple kind of emotional appeal.

IV *Enter Mitchell*

Often enough Lawson is content to put before us the minor characteristics of the bushmen, rather than the essential virtues with which he is dealing in these two stories. "Enter Mitchell" perhaps illustrates this aspect of his bush-writing best. I shall quote it in full, for there would be nothing left of its quality in a summary or selection. This is the first appearance in Lawson's work of the figure of Mitchell, a personality whom he used in a whole string of stories, almost all of them marked by a kind of ironic humor which Lawson handled very effectively. The story precisely renders the tone of the bushman's attitude to the townee: a touch of truculence, a wariness to resist the townsman's possibly disdainful attitude toward the unsophisticated rustic, but at the same time a relaxed confidence on the part of the bushman in the justice of his own claim to superiority. It conveys, too, with a precise rightness, the casual tone of the bushman, easy and drawling but not at all soft. The body droops in curves, but the line of the jaw is firm.

The Western train had just arrived at Redfern railway station with a lot of ordinary passengers and one swagman.

He was short, and stout, and bow-legged, and freckled, and sandy. He had red hair and small, twinkling, grey eyes, and—what often goes with such things—the expression of a born comedian. He was dressed in a ragged, well-washed print shirt, an old black waistcoat with a calico back, a pair of cloudy moleskins patched at the knees and held up by a plaited greenhide belt buckled loosely round his hips, a pair of well-worn, fuzzy blucher boots, and a soft felt hat, green with age, and with no brim worth mentioning, and no crown to speak of. He swung a swag on to the platform, shouldered it, pulled out a billy and water-bag, and then went to a dog-box in the brake van.

Five minutes later he appeared on the edge of the cab-platform, with an anxious-looking cattle-dog crouched against his legs, and one end of the chain in his hand. He eased down the swag against the post, turned his face to the city, tilted his hat forward, and scratched the well-developed back of his head with a little finger. He seemed undecided what track to take.

"Cab, sir!"

The swagman turned slowly and regarded cabby with a quiet grin.

"Now, do I look as if I want a cab?"

"Well, why not? No harm, anyway—I thought you might want a cab."

Swaggy scratched his head, reflectively.

"Well," he said, "you're the first man that has thought so these ten years. What do I want with a cab?"

"To go where you're going, of course."

"Do I look knocked up?"

"I didn't say you did."

"And I didn't say you said I did. . . . Now, I've been on the track this five years. I've tramped two thousan' miles since last Chris'mas, and I don't see why I can't tramp the last mile. Do you think my old dog wants a cab?"

The dog shivered and whimpered; he seemed to want to get away from the crowd.

"But then, you see, you ain't going to carry that swag through the streets, are you?" asked the cabman.

"Why not? Who'll stop me? There ain't no law agin it, I b'lieve?"

"But then, you see, it don't look well, you know."

"Ah! I thought we'd get to it at last."

The traveller up-ended his bluey against his knee, gave it an affectionate pat, and then straightened himself up and looked fixedly at the cabman.

"Now, look here!" he said, sternly and impressively, "can you see anything wrong with that old swag o' mine?"

It was a stout, dumpy swag, with a red blanket outside, patched with blue, and the edge of a blue blanket showing in the inner rings at the end. The swag might have been newer; it might have been cleaner; it might have been hooped with decent straps, instead of bits of clothes-line and greenhide—but otherwise there was nothing the matter with it, as swags go.

"I've humped that old swag for years," continued the bushman; "I've carried that old swag thousands of miles—as that old dog knows—an' no one ever bothered about the look of it, or of me, or of my old dog, neither; and do you think I'm going to be ashamed of that old swag, for a cabby or anyone else? Do you think I'm going to study anybody's feelings? No one ever studied mine! I'm in two minds to summon you for using insulting language towards me!"

He lifted the swag by the twisted towel which served for a shoulder-strap, swung it into the cab, got in himself and hauled the dog after him.

"You can drive me somewhere where I can leave my swag and dog while I get some decent clothes to see a tailor in," he said to the cabman. "My old dog ain't used to cabs, you see."

Then he added, reflectively: "I drove a cab myself, once, for five years in Sydney."

V *Bushman Frailties*

Lawson's estimate of the bushmen is not entirely, and therefore unconvincingly, eulogistic. Like most men of strong patriotic feeling, he can attack sharply where he finds weaknesses which threaten his people. Although he had an affection for the bushmen's casualness, he turns acridly critical when he finds the casualness degenerating into sluggishness of mind. In "A Day on a Selection," [11] for example, he assails the squalor of an Australian smallholding, arising from the indifferent ignorance of its owner. It is true that this selector is an Englishman, but Lawson is obviously suggesting that the conditions which he is here painting are characteristic of the country. Indeed, there is little point in the sketch unless it is intended to criticize a national weakness.

A similar defect is assailed in "Middleton's Rouseabout," one of the few poems in which Lawson employs the gift for succinct irony which he often displays in his prose:

Tall and freckled and sandy
  Face of a country lout;
This was the picture of Andy,
  Middleton's Rouseabout.

Type of a coming nation
  In the land of cattle and sheep;
Worked on Middleton's station,
  Pound a week and his keep.

On Middleton's wide dominions
  Plied the stockwhip and shears;
Hadn't any opinions,
  Hadn't any "idears."

Swiftly the years went over,
  Liquor and drought prevailed.
Middleton went as a drover,
  After his station had failed.

Type of a careless nation,
  Men who are soon played out,
Middleton was:—and his station
  Was bought by the Rouseabout.

Flourishing beard and sandy,
  Tall and solid and stout;
This is the picture of Andy,
  Middleton's Rouseabout.

Now on his own dominions
  Works with his overseers;
Hasn't any opinions,
  Hasn't any idears.[12]

VI *The Bushwomen*

Lawson is scarcely less concerned to present the women than the men of the bush, but there is a difference in the emphasis of his treatment. However tough the conditions, the men are usually spiritually victorious. Admiration is the dominant note in Lawson's celebration of them. With the women, there is a stronger emphasis on the note of pity. He understands that the loneliness of bush-life falls most heavily upon them and that the absence of the refinements of life affects them more deeply than the men. The tough life and the broiling burden of the sun render both men and women stringy and hard; but a stringy hardness may make a man look stronger—in a woman it is a withering. Lawson perceives all this with a deep compassion. In his later years he more than once recorded his pride that he had paid to the Bush-women their deserved tribute:

> Let this also be recorded when I've answered to the roll:
> That I pitied haggard women—wrote for them with all my
> soul.[13]

"The Drover's Wife," perhaps the best-known story which Lawson ever wrote (it is certainly the most widely anthologized), is representative of a whole group of compassionate portraits of the haggard women. Characteristically, Lawson conveys the pitiful elements in her life more effectively through its slighter details than through the dramatic episodes which it records (which include fighting a bushfire, attempting to save a farm dam in flood-time, and protecting her children from a snake which has taken up quarters beneath her house):

> All days are much the same to her; but on Sunday afternoon she dresses herself, tidies the children, smartens up baby, and goes for a lonely walk along the bush track, pushing an old perambulator in front of her. . . . There is nothing to see, however, and not a soul to meet.[14]

It would, however, be a mistake to dwell too much on the pity which Lawson's bushwomen inspire. Indeed it seems almost an impertinence to use such a word in reference to them. The final impression which they convey, like the men, is one of strength and of a spiritual victory. That victory is less assured than it is with the men. Something of the quality of the women has been eroded by the conditions under which they live; but in the last analysis they are to be admired more than pitied.

This admiration of bushman virtue was an effective expression of the prevailing Australian mythology of the time. The more critical elements in Lawson's view could be accepted as at least contributing to a sense of the importance of the bushman's figure and as guaranteeing the sincerity of the admiration.

VII *Mateship*

This contemporary feeling that Lawson's work was expressing the national ethos was greatly strengthened by the prominence in it of the theme of Mateship. I doubt if a eulogy has ever been pronounced on Lawson which did not use that word at least three times in the course of its exordium—and, as uttering eulogies of Lawson is a minor national industry, that association of the term with his name must have occurred some thousands of times. Indeed, Lawson carried his worship of the Mateship idea rather further than most bushmen did. For them it was the working basis of practical ethics; for him it was virtually a religion. It is the theme of dozens of his stories and verses. Again, however, it is often the incidental touches which convey the idea more significantly than the plots of the narrations. For example, in "Telling Mrs. Baker" there is an interchange when Andy forms his intention to visit the widow:

> "I'll have to face her—and you'll have to come with me."
> "Damned if I will," I said.
> "But you'll have to," said Andy. "You'll have to stick to me: you're surely not crawler enough to desert a mate in a case like this." [15]

What Lawson is here establishing is the discomfort which the drovers felt in performing their task of lying. He knows that he can make this clear by showing that it was the kind of emergency in which the sacred duty of Mateship could not be decently evaded.

In a lighter vein, there is a scrap of dialogue in "Shooting The Moon." The narrator has just told the story of a man's generously mately behavior:

> "Well, he was white any road."
> "Yes, I knew him well after that, and only heard one man say a word against him."

"And did you stoush him?"

"No; I was going to, but Tom wouldn't let me. He said he was frightened I might make a mess of it, and he did it himself." [16]

Again it is the assumption that tells; the listener's confident assurance that a good mate will be avenged by force of arms.

During the period of his decline, Lawson became obsessed with the Mateship theory. Sympathy with the unfortunate, expressed through a staunch generosity of action, seemed to him now almost the whole duty of man. Story after story is a variant of the parable of the Good Samaritan; but Lawson had now lost the delicacy of touch, the sure economic naturalistic simplicity, which had once made him an artist of the same type as St. Luke. He thumps out his Samaritanisms with an evangelical fervor, and the artistry, the sense of precise truthfulness, is lost in the sermonizing.

In his treatment of the Mateship theme, Lawson shows a breadth of tolerance which went far beyond that of the typical bushman. He cannot comfortably echo the nationalistic and class-conscious narrowness which restricted the bushman's mateships—in theory anyway. Ideologically, Lawson accepted the principle that the squatters were the "baddies" of the contemporary economic melodrama. He could assert it, in verse, in wide pugnacious generalizations. When, in the naturalistic detail of his stories, he must see them as individuals, a humanely sympathetic treatment gets the better of obedience to political mythology. The moment when Lawson most explicitly states the nature of the Mateship creed occurs in "Telling Mrs. Baker," to quote that story yet again:

> We could have started on the back track at once, but, drunk or sober, mad or sane, good or bad, it isn't bush religion to desert a mate in a hole; and the boss was a mate of ours; so we stuck to him.[17]

The *boss* was a mate. Socialism was only Mateship; but Mateship wasn't only Socialism. That touch is not accordant with the strict theory of the mythology; but I doubt if any bushman would have found anything in it which he could not accept.

Not that Lawson failed to understand and express the political version of the Mateship idea. There is a touch in the story "Lord Douglas" which nicely conveys its quality. Mitchell has been pretending to justify the character of Douglas (nicknamed "Lord"), who had the wrong political views (he was anti-union and employed a Chinese cook). One "Barcoo-Rot" takes Mitchell's irony literally, and comments:

> "You're allers findin' excuses for blacklegs and scabs, Mitchell," said Barcoo-Rot (who took Mitchell seriously, and would have taken a laughing jackass seriously). "Why you'd find a white spot on a squatter. I wouldn't be surprised if you black-legged yourself in the end."
>
> This was an unpardonable insult from a Union point of view, and the chaps half unconsciously made room on the floor for Barcoo-Rot to fall after Jack Mitchell hit him.

Lawson's continuation of the incident is, however, entirely characteristic of his personal approach to Mateship:

> But Mitchell took the insult philosophically.
>
> "Well, Barcoo-Rot," he said, nursing the other leg, "for the matter of that, I did find a white spot on a squatter once. He lent me a quid when I was hard-up. There's white spots on the blackest characters if you only drop prejudice and look close enough. I suppose even Jack-the-Ripper's character was speckled. Why, I can even see spots on your character, Barcoo-Rot. I've known white spots to spread on chaps' characters until they were little short of saints. Sometimes I even fancy I can feel my own wings sprouting. And as for turning blackleg—well I suppose I've got a bit of the crawler in my composition (most of us have), and a man never knows what might happen to his principles."
>
> "Well," said Barcoo-Rot, "I beg yer pardon. Ain't that enough?"
>
> "No," said Mitchell, "you ought to wear a three-bushel bag and ashes for three months, and drink water; but since the police would send you to an asylum if you did that, I think the best thing we can do is to go out and have a drink." [18]

Lawson fully accepted the principle that the working man should show an assertive independence of the employing class. In the pleasant verses "Andy's Gone with Cattle," he is expressing the district's sense of loss in the absence of Andy who is away on a droving trip:

> Who now shall wear the cheerful face
> In times when things are slackest?

And who shall whistle round the place
When Fortune frowns her blackest?

Oh, who shall cheek the squatter now
When he comes round us snarling?
His tongue is growing hotter now
Since Andy crossed the Darling.[19]

These are the only two personal qualities mentioned in the poem, in order to individualize the figure—the virtues of cheerfulness and disrespect for economic rank placed side by side to identify one of the "goodies."

Yet Lawson will not let such acceptances narrow the range of his human sympathies. He has given, I think, only one strongly individualized portrait of a squatter—that of Black in "Joe Wilson's Courtship." Even that is very brief, but it is a charming portrait. Lawson is careful to justify this affectionate treatment of one of the "baddies," in terms of the mythology, by mentioning that Black was "a squatter of the old school who had shared the early hardships of his men, and could not see why he should not shake hands and have a smoke and a yarn over old times with any of the old station-hands that happened to come along." [20]

The technical purpose of this passage is to prepare the way for a later effect. Lawson wants to convey to the reader that Black had learned the hard way that the realities of matrimony did not square with the confident hopes of young love. To convey this to the reader, he mentions that Black "married an Englishwoman after the hardships were over and she'd never got any Australian notions." He adds one confirming touch:

"Well, Joe, what is it? Do you want another job? If you do, you'll have to ask Mrs. Black or Bob" (Bob was his eldest son); "they're managing the station for me now, you know." He could be bitter sometimes in his quiet way.[21]

Writing for an Australian audience of his time, Lawson has now said enough to establish his point. Black was a squatter of the old school who liked to yarn with his men, married to an Englishwoman who hadn't got any Australian notions—poor chap.

VIII *View of Aliens*

Lawson could, indeed, carry his scorn for the English to an extremism which the bushmen shared. In "A Sketch of Mateship," he gives us a tiny discourse on the favorite theme declared in the title. Jim and Bill are returning to Bourke from a shearing job. They decide to sell a horse belonging to Bill, to provide more money for the spree which customarily marked the shearers' return from the enforced sobriety of the back country. Jim, being the better talker of the two, is sent ahead to do the bargaining. He succeeds in getting the good price of £8, but he is a bit annoyed with himself because more patient bargaining would have got him £10. The story continues:

> Pause. Bill sat waiting for him to hand the money over; but Jim withdrew his hand empty, stretched and said:
> "Ah, well, Bill, I done it in. Lend us a couple o' notes."
> Jim had been drinking and gambling all night and he'd lost the eight pounds as well as his own money.
> Bill didn't explode. What was the use? He should have known that Jim wasn't to be trusted with money in town. It was he who had been the fool. He sighed and lent Jim a pound, and they went in to have a drink.

But for once Lawson's sense of the right ending deserts him. He adds a moralistic paragraph:

> Now it strikes me that if this had happened in a civilised country (like England), Bill would have had Jim arrested and jailed for larceny as a bailee, or embezzlement, or whatever it was. And would Bill or Jim or the world have been any better for it?[22]

The injustice of this is rendered worse by the touch of self-righteousness. It was reasonable enough to assert and exemplify Mateship as a creed which had acquired a special force under the conditions of frontier living; it was absurdly unreasonable to assume that the English knew nothing of its elements. Incidentally, it was very poor practice of the religion which the story is preaching.

It would appear that this story was written after Lawson's visit to England (one can never be sure of the dating of a Lawson story, because *The Bulletin* often paid for one and held it in the files, sometimes for years, until it was convenient to publish it). If this is so, then the story is something of a throwback, for Lawson's acceptance of the Australian contempt for the English did not survive his visit to their country. Certainly, he continued to despise the feudal servility of the English villager. He had rented rooms in such a village and was therefore technically ranked there as a "Gentleman." He found it hard to take the locals' habit of addressing him as "Sir," even when they were guiding his wavering footsteps home from the pub. For the English in general, however, he acquired a considerable admiration and understanding sympathy, and he has defended them against the usual colonial charges in two pieces of prose.[23]

Perhaps more remarkable, in the setting of his time and his background, are his references to Italy—a country peopled, as the bushman saw it, by subhuman creatures known as Dagoes. Lawson (it is characteristic of the influences in his environment which largely made him) did not actively seek to make any cultural exploration of Europe on his trip abroad. He did, however, spend the day ashore when his ship called at Naples and at Genoa. Of the latter, he wrote a set of verses with the refrain: "The only city in the world/That I was loth to leave."[24] Moreover, in his account of it, he shows a discernment which one hardly expects from this uneducated rustic: "The rag that drapes a balcony/An artist's hands have hung." There is one other short passage in which Lawson has expressed his response to Italy:

> Wine-cellar in Italy: Italian posing—not the arrogant, insolent, you-be-knifed swagger of the Spaniard, but the we-are-happy, we-are-brothers, I-love-the-world pose of a son of Italy with wine in him, head well back, foot forward, wineglass held. Curve of arm and wrist artistically perfect. . . . Eyes shining and dancing: "Ello, Pietro there! How is it with Pietro! Good old Pietro! Here's to Pietro!" Brings glass down round to lips with a sweep, drinks, and sets glass on top of cask.[25]

Henry James knew Italy far better than Lawson did and was far better prepared by his education for its appreciation. Has he written any passage which so swiftly and surely reveals the essential quality of the people of that country?

The conflict between the mythology's demands and Lawson's

width of sympathy is perhaps more strikingly revealed in a remark about the Chinese:

> I have tried several times during my life to hate the Chinese and China: but, somehow, I never could—probably because our creeds were somewhat similar when I was young and China was old—and China was kind to me and mine in times of trouble.[26]

Lawson felt it was his duty to hate the Chinese because that was a part of the Bushman and *Bulletin* creed; his failure to achieve that patriotic duty was only partly due to the kindness to which he refers. Even without that motive, he would probably have failed to hate the individual members of a race which exemplifies those virtues of the affections he admired.

IX *Political Writing*

The popular feeling that Lawson voiced the aspirations of the Australian people was strengthened by the political writing of his earlier years, particularly the ballads in which he declaimed a radical insurgence. His general attitude toward social questions seems to have come from his mother; despite his emotional resentment of her lack of affection, he was strongly influenced by her intellectually. There may, too, have been some influence toward radical attitudes from his father. Two passages in Lawson's writing[27] seem to imply that Peter was a digger at Ballarat in 1854 and that he supported the agitation which led to the Eureka Stockade—an incident in which the miners took up arms in protest against the high taxes levied on them at a time when they were denied the franchise. The incident occupies a somewhat overemphasized position in Australian mythology because it was the only occasion when there was any armed rising on behalf of popular rights.

These influences were strengthened by the bitterness of his own early experiences, on that wretched selection, and, more searingly, during his early years in Sydney. In his autobiography, Lawson has written:

> I knew what it was, when I was out of work, for a few days in winter, to turn out shivering and to be down at the Herald office at four o'clock on bitter mornings, and be one of the haggard group striking matches and running down the "Wanted" column of the damp

sheets posted outside. I knew what it was to tramp long distances and be one of a hopeless crowd of applicants. I knew what it was to drift about the streets in patched and shabby clothes and feel furtive and criminal-like. I knew all that before I wrote "Faces in the Street"—before I was twenty. I knew what it was to go home to a cold, resentful, gloomy, and unbelieving welcome, and blind unreasoning reproaches at the very least.[28]

(The last sentence throws an interesting light on Lawson's relations with his mother.)

Lawson has said that he read the Socialistic propagandists and listened to their lectures: "I heard Tommy Walker and Collins, and the rest of 'em, and, of course, a host of Yankee free-thought and socialist lecturers." [29] It is doubtful if he pursued such studies very far or very deeply. The continuation of the passage I have just quoted more accurately conveys the tone of his response: "I wore the green in fancy, gathered at the rising of the moon, charged for the fair land of Poland, and dreamed of dying on the barricades to the roar of the 'Marseillaise'—for the Young Australian Republic." Lawson's political reactions were, indeed, almost entirely emotional in their nature. He felt a deep compassion for the oppressed victims of privilege and flared with righteous indignation on their (and his own) behalf, but his grasp of constructive policies of reform does not appear to have been firm.

There is, in fact, a discrepancy between the tone of Lawson's political verse and the tone of the Australian radical movement of the time. He could, upon occasion, detail the kind of reforms which were generally adumbrated, as he did in part of his reply to Paterson.[30] He was further allied to the movement by his confidence that the Australian community, and the bushmen in particular, would lead the revolt against privilege—a confidence expressed in such lines as "You'll triumph not in this land as you triumphed in the old" or "there are men of settled purpose in the regions of the West." [31] But on what seemed a more important issue, Lawson parted company with the essentially reformist nature of Australian radical policy. The Labour movement aimed first at strong unionism, with the strike as the weapon of ultimate resort, and later at the conquest of political power through electoral victory. The tenets of Marx played little part in forming the minds of Australian leftists of the time; they acclaimed, rather, such prophets as Henry George and Edward Bellamy.

Lawson's political verse does not usually support such an approach; it is frankly revolutionary. The most widely acclaimed of his ballads of protest was "Faces in the Street." It expresses the dismay of the country boy observing the gray hopelessness of the slum-dwellers of Sydney. He had known perhaps as grinding a poverty as theirs on the selection; but the men and women of Eurunderee had maintained a robustness, a spiritual resilience which the city dwellers had lost:

> I look in vain for traces of the fresh and fair and sweet
> In sallow, sunken faces that are drifting through the street
> Drifting on, drifting on,
> To the scrape of restless feet:
> I can sorrow for the owners of the faces in the street.

The conclusion to which this contemplation led Lawson was not the advocacy of reformist measures. "Faces in the Street" ends with exuberant declamation:

> Then, like a pent-up river that has broken bank and wall
> The human flood came pouring with the red flags over all,
> And kindled eyes all blazing bright with revolution's heat,
> And flashing swords reflecting rigid faces in the street—
> Pouring on, pouring on,
> To a drum's loud threatening beat,
> And the war-hymns and the cheering of the people in the street.
>
> And so it must be while the world goes rolling round its course
> The warning pen shall write in vain, the warning voice grow hoarse,
> For not until a city feels Red Revolution's feet
> Shall its sad people miss awhile the terrors of the street—
> The dreadful everlasting strife
> For scarcely clothes and meat
> In that pent track of living death—the city's cruel street.[32]

This is not an isolated extremism. "Freedom on the Wallaby" makes a similar declaration:

> So we must fly a rebel flag
> As others did before us,

And we must sing a rebel song
    And join in rebel chorus.
We'll make the tyrants feel the sting
    Of those that they would throttle;
They needn't say the fault is ours
    If blood should stain the wattle.[33]

In "The Army of the Rear," a ballad which Lawson said "went through the U.S." [34] he writes:

The wealthy care not for our wants, nor for the pangs we feel,
Our hands have clutched in vain for bread, and now they clutch for steel.
Come, men of rags and hunger, come! There's work for heroes here!
There's room still in the vanguard of the Army of the Rear! [35]

Intriguingly to the after-observer, this difference of view on an essential issue does not seem to have troubled Lawson's radical admirers of the time. I have read dozens of eulogies of his social championship, most of them written by his contemporaries, but I can recall encountering only one disclaimer of his extremism. It was enough, apparently, that he expressed the emotions underlying their political enthusiasms and that he shared their confidence in the ability of the Australians to lead the way to a Socialist Utopia. A mere difference of opinion whether the ballot box or the barricades should be the instrument used for its attainment did not seem to them important. This indifference suggests to us both the naïveté and the intransigence of spirit of the radical enthusiasms of the Australians of the nineties.

There is one political poem, written by Lawson in his earlier years, which causes some embarrassment to his leftist admirers of today (who make something of a fetish-figure of Lawson). "The Star of Australasia" is not an easy poem for them to ignore, for it is one of the most effective of his ballads, with a convincing vigor of movement and a clean-cut vividness in its incidental pictures; but it declares a conviction which no modern leftist—and few moderns of any political affiliation—can support:

We boast no more of our bloodless flag that rose from a nation's slime;

Better a shred of a deep-dyed flag from the storms of the olden time.
From grander clouds in our peaceful skies than ever were there before
I tell you the Star of the South shall rise in the lurid clouds of war.
It ever must be while blood is warm and the sons of men increase
For ever the nations rose in storm, to rot in a deadly peace.

. . . .

And many a rickety son of a gun, on the tides of the future tossed,
Will tell how battles were really won that History says were lost,
Will trace the field with his pipe, and shirk the facts that are hard to explain,
As grey old mates of the diggings work the old ground over again . . .[36]

This Kipling-like sentiment[37] is the more embarrassing to radicals because the poem has a claim to prophetic accuracy. The Australian sense of nationhood and of maturity was strongly advanced by the community's pride in the reputation won by her soldiers in World War I.

The radicals of the nineties probably found nothing to worry them in the poem. Nationalism and Socialism were inextricably interwoven in their ideology, and a sense of the horror of war was not widespread in any nineteenth-century community. They probably found the ballad an acceptable expression of the ebullient confidence in the Australian vitality on which their Utopian hopes were based. Modern readers, apart from the embarrassed radicals, may find in it a significance of a different kind. When one sets it beside Lawson's ballads of "red" revolution, one recognizes a common trait: a subconscious longing for the release of tensions through violence. It is an unexpected trait to find in this pacific individual who shrank from involvement in a fist-fight and whose work so frequently celebrates the virtues of compassion, sensitivity and tenderness. Yet it is clearly present in these ballads and in certain others, notably those which look back nostalgically to the spacious days of romance:

Then a man could fight if his heart were bold, and win if his faith were true—

Were it love, or honor, or power, or gold, or all that our
hearts pursue;
Could live to the world for the family name, or die for the
family pride,
Could flee from sorrow and wrong and shame in the days
when the world was wide.[38]

Somewhere enclosed in this admirer of the gentler qualities was a wouldbe swashbuckler.

The rash fierce blaze of riot of Lawson's political writing did not last; most of it was composed before he was twenty-seven. He never lost his sympathy with radical aspirations, indeed his championship of the social rejects intensified, although its emphasis changed to a simple demand for charity of mind; but he rapidly lost interest or faith in political action, whether revolutionary or reformist. In his electoral testimonial for Thomas Mutch (see p. 55), Lawson writes, "I don't agree with anybody's politics." Elsewhere he declared:

I have written about these things before, many times—and to little purpose, I think now. There was a time—when I was younger, and madder, and "narrower," and more ignorant of the world, more sincere and loyal to man, and braver and truer-hearted than I am now—when I dreamed of barricades and a red death for the sake of right and justice, and all that sort of thing, and wrote about it, too, in prose and rhyme. But now I don't think I'd live for a week under the freedom or tyranny of Unionism, universal brotherhood, glorious liberty, or whatever you like to call it, provided I could get out of the land of freedom inside the said week.[39]

In his later years Lawson retreated—or progressed—to more conservative and conventional views which have not weathered well. The formerly spirited opponent of the Imperial connection became, during World War I, a patriot of the more tawdry kind, British rather than Australian, and quite unperceptive of the tragic follies of a society which could find no alternative to mass slaughter. Readers may interpret this change according to their lights. Conservatives will find in it the proper maturing of youthful exuberance under the influence of experience. Liberals may prefer to believe that his later utterances declare, not the "real

Lawson," but the gallons of beer in which he had been drowned. Lawson himself, to judge by certain morose and sometimes maudlin self-examinations, sorrowfully accepted the second interpretation.

CHAPTER 4

The Personal View

EVERY writer is in some measure the child of his age. He cannot escape the influence of the ideas which move and grow about him. Many writers—and Lawson was one of these—are proud declarers of the ideologies of the community to which they belong, defining the forward edge of its movement through time. But every writer of worth is also intensely himself. His artistic conceptions well up from the depths of his own experience and temperament. Often these two sources of influence, the internal and the external, create a tension which can both enrich and confuse the work of writers. Lawson was also one of these.

The preceding chapter has, I hope, shown how fully Lawson represented the Australian ethos of his time, despite occasional variations from it which I have indicated. Yet, at one important point, at least, he was out of touch with its prevailing tone. The mythical Australian of the nineties was essentially confident. He was naïvely but tenaciously convinced that he was the man of the future, pioneering the trail which led to Utopia. He knew that tough battles against his present oppressors still had to be fought, but he had little doubt of the outcome.

Lawson often enough declares this attitude. Moreover, he deeply admired not only the confidence but the easy good nature which he found in the bushman (although he was also aware of converse qualities). The phrase "cheerful grin" must occur dozens of times in his stories, often linked to some such term as "scallawag," affectionately indicating an element of moral carelessness in the subject of the portrait. But, while he admired this cheerfulness, he was far from sharing it himself. His temperament was deeply melancholic, for reasons which the reader of my second chapter will have little difficulty in assessing. That melancholy is ultimately the strongest influence on his work, despite the sentimental tendency which also marks it—and, in its later phases, disfigures it.

I *Sentiment*

At this point a digression seems to be advisable; for we have stumbled upon the term "sentimental," and, if we are to use it in company, we need to come to terms with it. It is an awkward word, all the more because it happens to be two words. There is "sentiment" which is comparatively respectable, and there is "sentimentality" which is a term of abuse. For each of these, "sentimental" is the adjectival representative.

This is not the only complexity. What is the difference between "sentiment" and "sentimentality"? Is it merely a matter of degree and of subjective response? Do we use them as we use the words "sweet" and "sugary," saying "sentiment" when there is about as much as we can comfortably take and "sentimentality" when there is so much of it that it makes us sick? Perhaps we often do; yet we feel that there is a qualitative, rather than a quantitative difference between them. Sentiment, it seems to me, is the expression of a scale of values which prefers the tendernesses of human response to the virilities, the softnesses to the strengths. The man of sentiment will incidentally prefer the emotional to the intellectual. Sentimentalism is the indulgence in that emotionalism for its own sake and at the expense of truth. Example reveals more than definition, and the revealing example here is Mozart's music—full of sentiment and unerringly avoiding sentimentality.

You will observe that, in terms of my definition, sentimentality is not merely an overextension of sentiment, the Aristotelian extreme of the virtuous mean (if sentiment is a virtue). It is different in kind. We use for the one quality a word derived from the other because sentimentality is the besetting temptation to which the man of sentiment is exposed.

Lawson was certainly a man of sentiment. He had a tenacious regard for the tendernesses of human response, and he seems scarcely interested in most of the virilities, save in those ballads which express the "would-be swashbuckler." He is also often a sentimentalist in much of his verse and in his later prose. The quality does occur, too, in the prose of the good period, but remarkably little for a writer so exposed to temptation by the strength of his sentiment. To return to the point of departure of this necessary digression, let us look in some detail at the melancholic element in Lawson's writing.

II *The Melancholy Landscape*

This is revealed in many facets of his work. There is the dismal tone, insistently recurrent, of his landscape settings. One could assemble a sizable anthology of such passages as these:

> The country looks just as bad for a hundred miles round Hungerford, and beyond that it gets worse—a blasted, barren wilderness that doesn't even howl. If it howled, it would be a relief.[1]

> A hot, breathless, blinding sunrise—the sun having appeared suddenly above the ragged edge of the barren scrub like a great disc of molten steel. No hint of a morning breeze before it, no sign of earth or sky to show that it is morning—save the position of the sun.[2]

> It was blazing hot outside and smothering hot inside the weatherboard and tin shanty at Dead Dingo, a place on the cleared road, where there was a pub and a police station, and which was sometimes called "Roasted" and other times "Potted-Dingo"—nicknames suggested by the everlasting drought and the vicinity of the one-pub township of Tinned Dog.[3]

Against these one can set one celebration of the splendors of the Australian scene, written in London under the influence of nostalgia, and cast in a rhetorical style uncharacteristic of Lawson.[4] There is, too, a short lyrical passage used to set the atmosphere for Joe Wilson's proposal,[5] and that is about all. If one assembled the meteorological statistics, one would probably find that the total rainfall in the collected works of Henry Lawson was about three inches. Once, indeed, the drought does break in the Bourke country. It must have been an occasion to set the locals caroling hymns of praise. Does Lawson? No! "In a Wet Season"[6] is a superbly accurate delineation of a misery of dampness, as dismal as Lawson's more customary pictures of drought.

It may be argued—it often has been—that the Australian scenes which Lawson best knew, about Eurunderee and Bourke, *are* dismal, that Lawson was merely setting down what was there to be seen. True, no doubt; but when a man really knows a countryside, when it has seeped into his blood, he usually finds in it elements of beauty, and, if he is a writer, he wants to communicate his sense of its beauty. Lawson's love of Australia was certainly deep, but it hardly colors at all his picture of the Australian scene. Studying Lawson's work, one becomes progressively more convinced that he was not merely objectively delineating the New South Wales plains; he was projecting onto them the landscape of his own soul.

III *Melancholy Self-Portrayal*

There is a virtual admission of this in the view of himself which Lawson often presents. I have written elsewhere that "Lawson, as unassumingly humble a writer as ever lived, knew very well that he belonged to the tragic élite of the sensitive." [7] I might have added that he consistently regarded this as his curse. There is almost a refrain through his work of such remarks as this:

I wasn't a healthy-minded average boy: I reckon I was born for a poet by mistake, and grew up to be a bushman, and didn't know what was the matter with me—or the world.[8]

I often think how at sunset, the past must come home to a new-chum black sheep, sent out to Australia and drifted into the bush. I used to think that they couldn't have much brains, or the loneliness would drive them mad.[9]

They all seemed to forget him as we entered the Heads; they had their own troubles to attend to. . . . But I didn't forget him. I wish sometimes that I didn't take such notice of things.[10]

There is another kind of remark that beats below the surface of Lawson's work:

The procession numbered fifteen, fourteen souls following the broken shell of a soul. Perhaps not one of the fourteen possessed a soul any more than the corpse did—but that doesn't matter.[11]

If we saw our married lives as others see them, half of us would get divorced.[12]

A man doesn't shoot himself when he's going to be made a lawful father for the first time, unless he can see a long way into the future.[13]

Taken in isolation, these comments suggest a man of cynical temperament. Such an interpretation of Lawson is, of course, wildly absurd. They express rather a profound melancholy, shaped into the irony which Lawson used to stiffen himself to endurance.

There are also thematic exemplifications of Lawson's gloom—for example, the frequent dwelling on the subject of death. This was already so marked in his early work that Paterson used it derisively in his set-to with Lawson in 1892:

> Now, for instance, Mr. Lawson—well of course, we almost cried.
> At the sorrowful description of how "little Arvie" died;
> And we lachrymosed in silence when "His Father's Mate" was slain;
> Then he went and killed the father, and we had to weep again.
> Ben Duggan and Jack Denver, too, he caused them to expire,
> After which he cooked the gander of Jack Dunn of Nevertire;
> And no doubt the bush is wretched if you judge it by the groan
> Of the sad and soulful poet with a graveyard of his own.[14]

IV *The Guilt Theme*

There is a far more significant recurrent theme in Lawson's work: the theme of a man loaded with a guilty past. He bears it usually with nobility, and with a growth in tenderness, and he is always sympathetically presented. There is Bogg of Geebung,[15] the derelict remittance-man with a broken love affair long ago, who ends in the river. There is the Oracle [16] who has caused the death of the woman he loved; there is the Hero of Redclay [17] who has gone to gaol on a false accusation because he has seduced a decent girl, and can only defend himself by revealing his presence in her bedroom. There is Doc Wilde, a character who appears to be a refugee from a Bret Harte story, and who is frequently and effectively used by Lawson. He is a Californian (Lawson calls him a Yankee, but this appears to be due to Australian ignorance of the niceties of American terminology), a doctor with high degrees, great skill and a penetrative shrewdness. He has killed a man in a row about a girl and has subsequently drifted to an

Australian bush practice where he assuages his despair with whiskey, an outward cynicism, and acts of kindness.[18] There is Peter M'Laughlan, a lay preacher who delivers unconventional sermons to the bush people in their own language, with great effect. Lawson uses him as the central figure in several of his later stories of Samaritanism. His saintliness and understanding, it is ultimately revealed, are created by the memory of early guilt (again connected with a girl).[19]

Perhaps the most effective of all stories on this theme is "The Babies in the Bush." In it we are first introduced to Walter Head, a boss drover, a reserved, gloomy man who has nevertheless an aura of gentleness and depth of feeling. An intuitive sympathy grows between him and Jack Ellis, the narrator of the story. Eventually, Head invites Ellis to visit his home and meet his wife. There is obviously something queer about her. She is nearing middle age, but appears quite young, almost childish, and she has an innocent charm. After supper, Mrs. Head begins to talk of her children, to show their photographs. Then she tells Jack how they were lost in the bush and never found. But she knows that all is well. The reason the search parties did not track the youngsters successfully must be because the Bush Fairies took charge of them, as they do with lost children. They are bringing them back home next year. Head humors his wife's delusion with a grave and skilful devotion.

There is a second guest present, who had worked on Head's sheep-station in the days when the present drover had owned one. When he and Jack Ellis are alone, he fills in some of the details. After the loss of the children, Mrs. Head had been "raving mad" for some months. She eventually emerged from the asylum able to face life with the support of her delusion, but incapable of maturing. Head had spent all he had on unsuccessful consultations with specialists in mental disease. At last he has had to accept the situation. The last touch is added when, the next morning, Head makes his confession to Ellis:

"I was away when the children were lost, Jack. I used to go on a howling spree every six or nine months. Maggie never knew. I'd tell her I had to go to Sydney on business, or outback to look after some stock. When the children were lost, and for nearly a fortnight after, I was beastly drunk in an out-of-the-way shanty in the bush—a sly-grog shop. The old brute that kept it was too true to me. He thought that the story of the lost children was a trick to get me home, and he swore that he hadn't seen me. He never told me. I could have found those children, Jack. They were mostly new chums and fools about the run, and not one of the three policemen was a bushman. I knew those scrubs better than any man in the country." [20]

Perhaps the nature of Lawson's view of life is better suggested in two of his stories which stand together in the *While the Billy Boils* volume. The first is "The Union Buries Its Dead." Today it is regarded as one of Lawson's finest achievements, although it is one of his earliest stories. Perhaps the most remarkable thing about it is that it ever got itself written in the Australia of the 1890's; for in its implicit view of the nature of literature, in its manner and method, it is a mid-twentieth–century story. It is barely credible that it could have been written so long before the general establishment of its kind of literary approach, by an unschooled youth of twenty-four with no theories about his art. It only becomes credible if we assume that the story was forced upon Lawson by a profound need to shape what it declares.

It is a story quite without plot. In an outback township, a traveler, taking horses through, has been drowned while fording a river. He is almost unknown in the township, but he has been a good union man, and is therefore entitled to fraternal gestures of respect. The story simply describes his funeral. In the modern manner, it is built up from a series of details, selected and toned so as to evoke an emotional response, to suggest an interpretation of the incident as a symbol of the quality of the human experience (Lawson, of course, certainly never thus described, or recognized, his intention, and would have rejected such a description with scorn—he once had to be forcibly held in his chair while a lecturer was discoursing on his writings).[21]

Many of the details used are flavored with a satiric irony:

> The departed was a Roman and the majority of the town were otherwise—but unionism is stronger than creed. Liquor, however, is stronger than unionism; and, when the hearse presently arrived, more than two-thirds of the funeral were unable to follow. . . .
> On the way to the cemetery we passed three shearers sitting on the shady side of a fence. One was drunk—very drunk. The other two cov-

ered their right ears with their hats, out of respect for the departed—whoever he might have been—and one of them kicked the drunk and muttered something to him.

He straightened himself up, stared, and reached helplessly for his hat, which he shoved half off and then on again. Then he made a great effort to pull himself together—and succeeded. He stood up, braced his back against the fence, knocked off his hat, and remorsefully placed his foot on it—to keep it off his head till the funeral passed.[22]

Such touches could, I suppose, be technically described as "humorous." In isolation, they may even seem so. As Lawson uses them, they fall like a lash.

Overenthusiastic disciples of the mythology have attempted to see "The Union Buries Its Dead" as an expression of the Mateship theme, because of the loyalty of the (sober) unionists. Its real purpose is almost the reverse—to declare the loneliness of the human condition and the deadliness of human indifference. One may judge Lawson's subjective intention by the touch with which he has chosen to end the story:

. . . It turned out afterwards that "James Tyson" wasn't his real name—only "the name he went by." . . .

We did hear, later on, what his real name was; but if we ever chance to read it in the "Missing Friends Column" we shall not be able to give any information to heart-broken mother or sister or wife, nor to anyone who could let him hear something to his advantage—for we have already forgotten the name.

The story which immediately follows "The Union" is very short—a mere 500 words—and apparently trivial. Yet I believe that it is one of the most significant declarations of Lawson's attitude to life. It is called "On the Edge of the Plain." Mitchell and a friend are tramping the dry country in the hot season. They pause to rest in one of the rare bits of shade, and Mitchell tends a puppy which has been following at his heels, pouring a drink for it into the dented crown of his hat, examining its paws to see if it is fit to continue on foot. As he thus works, and intermittently comments on the puppy, he yarns, recalling the occasion when he returned home to find that his family had been told that he was dead. He describes, with humor, their initial consternation, then the joyful excitement of the reunion, and how his mother made him swear on the Bible never to leave home again. Then comes the ironic twist, typical of the Mitchell stories. His mate comments that he has broken his promise:

> Mitchell, stood up, stretched himself, and looked dolefully from his heavy swag to the wide, hot, shadeless cotton-bush plain ahead.
> "Oh, yes," he yawned, "I stopped at home for a week, and then they began to growl because I couldn't get any work to do."

There follows the characteristic prolonging echo of a Lawson story's ending:

> The mate guffawed and Mitchell grinned. They shouldered the swags, with the pup on top of Mitchell's, took up their billies and water-bags, turned their unshaven faces to the wide, hazy distance, and left the timber behind them.[23]

Let me emphasize that the story is called "On the Edge of the Plain." It is an improbable title. The plain is merely the setting in which Mitchell relates the episode. Can we believe that Lawson would have chosen this title if the story's tailpiece had not had a compelling significance for him? Indeed, it does give that sketch a depth which only Lawson could have achieved with such material. Two men, bearing the burden of the ironic and painful past, assuaging each other's loneliness, as they face the drought-stricken deadliness of a plain: here is a revealing symbol of Lawson's view of the human condition.

V *Reactions to Lawson's Melancholy*

His contemporaries were, of course, aware of the melancholy streak in his writings and sometimes attacked him for it, as the lines I have quoted from Paterson indicate. There is an essential injustice about such attacks, for the crime which it arraigns is no crime. A writer is entitled to express as dark a view of life as his experience, or his digestion, may impose upon him, provided that he conveys it with truth and imaginative vitality, as Lawson certainly does.

No doubt the detractors were moved partly by the uncomfortableness of Lawson's attitude, which was disconcerting to simple minds, partly by the feeling that his gloom betrayed the confident

Australianism of which he was an admired representative. But they had a more legitimate justification. There is something not quite right about his melancholy. A flavor of defeatism tinges it. It is too surrendering, it won't hit back at the fate with the loaded dice, against which Lawson feels that man is pitted. That obsession with the figure of the man with a guilty past—I do not think it arises because Lawson himself felt a sense of guilt, although that explanation is possible. I believe that he used that figure because the guilty man is impelled to a sympathy with the defeated.

Despite his talk of the blood upon the wattle, Lawson lacked the temperament of the rebel. He suggests too much the figure of Hamlet as (wrongly) interpreted by Coleridge. Moreover, as I have said, Lawson was usually indifferent to the virilities of human response—too indifferent to achieve a balanced view of life. He often suggests to us the attitude of Gorki; but he was incapable of that acceptance of the brutalities of instinctual response which gives perspective to the Russian's tenderness. To put it bluntly, Lawson hadn't quite got the guts which a writer needs.

He was aware of this. The figure of Joe Wilson is, or became, largely a self-portrait. That is the point of the remark in the postscript to the series of stories about him, "I know Joe Wilson very well." Lawson also remarks, "I had an idea of making Joe Wilson a strong character. Whether he is or not, the reader must judge. It seems to me that the man's sentimental selfishness, good-nature, 'softness' or weakness—call it what you like—developed as I wrote on." [24]

Those who were upset by Lawson's pessimism often preferred to minimize it rather than to attack it. Often these apologists point to his humor as a counterbalance to his gloom. It is true enough that Lawson was a humorist, and a balanced view of his work must take account of that fact. At least two of his comic tales—"The Loaded Dog" and "Bill, the Ventriloquial Rooster" [25]—are classics of their homely kind. More important, to my mind, are the incidental touches which often lighten, and sometimes deepen, the effect of his graver tales. These touches are usually less grim than the two passages I have quoted from "The Union Buries Its Dead." Nevertheless, those passages well convey the ironic dryness of the Lawsonian humor, and the quizzical observingness on which it is based.

Though this humor is certainly pervasive, to cite it as a defense against the charge of gloom is unconvincing. Behind such a defense lies the assumption that the antonym of "humorous" is "serious" or "sad." That is not true. The real antonym is "solemn." As Lawson himself said, "there seems a quiet sort of sadness always running through outback humor—whether alleged or otherwise."[26] This is true of more than the outback variety of humor. A comic writer may be as desperate as Swift, as melancholy as Thurber, as depressed as Zoschenko. A quiet sort of gloom does run through most of Lawson's humor.

VI *The Resolution of Conflict*

It will probably have occurred to the reader that there is almost a contradiction between the Lawson of the last chapter and the Lawson I have presented in this. There was certainly a measure of tension between the two personae—the Australian mythologist and "the grey dreamer," as Denton Prout calls him. But there is also an aspect of Lawson's writing which goes far to resolve the conflict between the two attitudes. Before I discuss that aspect, let me first establish an element which affects the lighting of the Lawsonian picture.

Despite his sense of the pain and loneliness of existence, Lawson never attempts to present to us the tragic view of life. That is only partly because he lacked the passion and the feeling for the virilities which the tragic presentation needs. Lawson was never articulate about ideas, and one is therefore forced to speak for him with an impertinent overconfidence. As I see it, then, he did not merely fail to reach the tragic view. He positively rejected it. Had he been capable of abstract expression, I think he might have said that the tragic view was a sentimentalism, sacrificing truth to the indulgence of emotionalism.

It is a view for which there is something to be said. In "On the Edge of the Plain," Mitchell knew the bitterness of exile, but not the relief of the tragic confrontation of it. He put the pup on the swag and walked on. And what he walked upon was a plain—that is an essential part of the symbol. For Lawson, the un-tragic tragedy of life is that it has not the satisfaction of peaks, however grim. For that reason, I believe that a naturalistic literary technique was not adopted by Lawson simply because it was generally used by his Australian contemporaries. He could, when he liked, be strikingly original and self-reliant in his development of techniques. If he was satisfied to accept the naturalistic mode, it was because he needed it to reflect his attitude to life. His conceptions demanded that he keep within the scale of life-as-it-is-lived.

The abstractions of the critical vocabulary are too flavorless to convey this point expressively. I shall, therefore, approach it obliquely. In introducing *King Lear* to students, I have sometimes said something like this: "This is not essentially a play about a great king in a barbaric age. Go into a hundred suburban homes at random, and in one of them you are likely to find the play of *Lear* enacting itself. There is Joe O'Leary, a bossy old chap who has created a good business as a master builder. He's old and tired now, so he retires and makes the business over to his two daughters to avoid death duties. He is going to live with each of them in turn. But he's a difficult old chap, and they are tougher types than he realizes. He spoils the grandchildren, interfering with maternal discipline. He wants his meals when he wants them, and that upsets domestic routine. He invites his old cronies in for beer parties, and other peoples' beer parties in your own home are hard to take. So the two daughters get together to present an ultimatum: either he does what he's told or he can go to the Old Men's Home."

So far, so good, and one can press the analogy quite a bit further—but not too far. There are things in *Lear* which cannot be thus translated. Joe O'Leary does not grandly curse his daughters; he declines into lachrymose querulousness. He does not achieve an insanity which illuminates the world by lightning flashes; he goes, rather tryingly, soft in the head.

What Shakespeare has done, for valid artistic purposes, is to enlarge the scale from living-as-it-is. That change has enabled him to illuminate certain truths better than the naturalistic scale could, but it has entailed also certain losses. As I have tried to suggest, in changing the scale, Shakespeare has changed the quality, too, of the experience. The element of truth which Shakespeare thus lost —and which was not needed for his kind of vision—was important to the Lawsonian conception. It was necessary for him to keep the scale of living-as-it-is, and he evolved his delicate and original technique in the light of this need. If the man who passed as James Tyson were elevated to the eminence of a Lear, he would lose all his power to move us.

Let me illustrate the point through a passage from the final Joe

Wilson story, in which Lawson is preparing for its climactic episode of Joe's purchase of a double-buggy, a status symbol of the time for which his wife hankers:

"I thought of getting the turn-out while she was laid up, keeping it dark from her until she was on her feet, and then showing her the buggy standing in the shed. But she had a bad time, and I had to have the doctor regularly, and get a proper nurse, and a lot of things extra; so the buggy idea was knocked on the head. I was set on it too: I'd thought of how, when Mary was up and getting strong, I'd say one morning, 'Go round and have a look in the shed, Mary; I've got a few fowls for you,' or something like that—and follow her round to watch her eyes when she saw the buggy. I never told Mary about that—it wouldn't have done any good." [27]

Trivial, you may think, merely sentimentalist. No; Lawson is here saying in effect: "Depth of emotion is not truthfully recorded through such expressions as the rhetoric of *Antony and Cleopatra.* Those who know the actuality of living know that it is on this scale that we feel most deeply."

Tucking into the backs of our minds this recognition of the scale of living-as-it-is, let us return to our consideration of the resolution of the conflict in his work. It is achieved through his emphasis on the virtue of endurance. Lawson, Heaven knows, was himself no stoic, but he thoroughly understood and admired the bushmen's stoicism. As he displays it to us, it is not a force which goes on the offensive. It does not meet and subdue the fate with the loaded dice. But it is not negative; it is not satisfied with mere survival. It has its positive aim and its moderate triumph.

To understand that aim we must return to Lawson, the man of sentiment, the convinced believer in the value of the tendernesses. Here lies the aim and the triumph of his stoics. Against all the odds, they maintain the value of the tendernesses. Under the pain, the loneliness, and the burden of guilt, they summon their strength in order to preserve unhardened hearts.

Lawson was, of course, aware that the common man often fails to maintain the tendernesses, and the sensitivity from which they spring. John le Gay Brereton tells a story of the early days of his almost lifelong friendship with Lawson. Brereton had been airing his radical Australian enthusiasms. Lawson broke in, "You know, I can't write all I think. My living partly depends on what I'm writing for *The Worker*. You can take it from me, Jack, the Australian worker is a brute, and nothing else." [28]

If one accepts this dictum literally, it is a shattering story. The success of Lawson, at least in his prose, largely depends on the sense of sincerity he creates. If he was, in fact, a commercially motivated liar, he was almost nothing as a writer. One cannot, however, accept it literally. There is too much in Lawson's work which denies it, and which can have had no commercial motive.

No doubt he said it. No doubt he almost meant it at the time—he was a man of moods as well as a moody man. The truth which Lawson was here exaggerating, he has expressed often enough in his writing. Although he regarded sensitiveness as his curse, he also knew that it was the spring from which he drew as a writer; he equates it with being a poet. As with most artists, sensitiveness was for him a basic human value, and he was correspondingly disappointed when he saw it fail in others. He was both idealistic and melancholic; consequently such disappointments could plunge him into ocean depths of dismay. Again and again, he records, in some sharp ironic comment, his anger at the failure in men of the sensitive response. The two passages which I have quoted from "The Union Buries Its Dead" represent a recurrent insistence in his work. It is implicit, for example, in his reference to "Bush-humour, alleged and otherwise." But he also knew, in less depressed moments, that the bushman at his best retained his sensitiveness of response, and he had expressed his admiration of that achievement in the way which I have tried to define.

One could cite many stories which declare this theme. "A Hero in Dingo Flats" is an obvious example. It is more subtly conveyed in the *Joe Wilson* series of stories, which I shall reserve for discussion in the next chapter. It is the theme of "Going Blind," one of those plotless little studies which Lawson handles so well. It is a portrait of an elderly bushman encountered in a seedy city boarding house. The old man has almost lost his sight. Each detail in the story is selected to suggest his undemonstrative fortitude, the failure of misfortune to make any inroads on his sweetness of nature. When things are looking black for the old man—he is practicing playing tunes on his concertina "in case the worst come to the worst"—a brother turns up from the country. It is clear that he is now in gentle and staunch hands. The two depart for their home, and Lawson ends with the sentence, "I felt their grips on my hand for five minutes after we parted." [29]

There is also, of course, Andy in "Telling Mrs. Baker" who "could keep a promise and nothing else" and who endured what was for him the repulsive task of telling a woman a pack of lies because that was what loyalty and human decency demanded. An absurdly slight example, you may think, of triumphant stoicism. Or is it rather an admirable example of Lawson's skill in retaining the scale of living-as-it-is?

Observe a detail in the symbolism of "On the Edge of the Plain" —on Mitchell's heavy swag, there rides a puppy.

These stories particularly well illustrate a central truth about Lawson. The needed modification of his desperate view of the human condition was provided by his sentiment, his sense of the insecurely triumphant survival of tenderness through endurance. The sentiment is the more convincing because of the rigor with which Lawson keeps within the scale of living-as-it-is. It is the more impressive and moving because it was formed within the matrix of a defeated man's dark melancholy.

CHAPTER 5

The Craftsman

IT WAS long customary to regard Lawson as a "natural" among writers. Here was an untutored son of the people who spoke the simple truths of the heart, without the mediation—or the distortion—of literary art. It was an interpretation which had a special appeal to the inheritors of the Australian mythology.

It is, I believe, a false view, and it implies an indirect tribute to the subtle masteries of Lawson's craftmanship. Had he been in truth as artless as his admirers believed, he would scarcely have been noticed. A simple warmth of heart, the precise observingness of his eye—these are the qualities upon which his appeal is ultimately based. But his work would never have reached its mark if those qualities had not been supported, in his best writing, by the shrewd economy and the originality of his artistry.

I *Lawson's "Best"*

His best writing: it is a proviso which the critic usually needs to make before he can justly analyze a writer's achievement. With Lawson, however, it means the exclusion of an unusually high proportion of his production, as high, perhaps, as a reader must make before the genius of Wordsworth stands clear. One must exclude, first, most of Lawson's verse; then one must disregard most of the prose he published after 1901. This leaves us with three volumes containing 103 short stories and sketches, and by no means all of these show Lawson exercising the qualities that make him a master. It seems a pitifully frail basis on which to rest a claim to mastery, particularly when there is so large a heap of dross from the same source; but gold mines usually assay in terms of pennyweights to the ton. After all, Melville's assured claim to greatness rests virtually on one novel and one short story.

An unevenness in Lawson's work is not unexpected, apart from the influence of those factors which led to his decline after 1900.

As I have said, he liked to work with a patient, measured deliberation. He could seldom command conditions which made this possible. In the letter to Lord Beauchamp in which he explained his reasons for wishing to escape to England, he wrote: "Because of the reputation I have gained in Australia, I am forced to sign hurried work—else I couldn't get it published at all. That's the cruellest part of the business." [1] Much of this hurried work was not republished in Lawson's books, but some of it slipped into them to give them bulk.

Lawson did not acquire his technical skill by the usual method of studying the works of masters; indeed, the belief that he was a "natural" is true in the sense that any such process would probably have destroyed his individual quality. He was not an extensive reader. His two great admirations were for Dickens and Bret Harte. The former was the more lasting enthusiasm, but it had little observable effect on his writing, save as it tempted him to sentimental indulgences. Lawson's humor is dry and ironic, quite unlike Dickens' genial, robust inventiveness. His art is based on precise observation and has nothing in common with Dickens' imaginative expansion of reality. From Bret Harte, Lawson probably learned something about the control of a story's movement; but there is no close resemblance between their methods.

II *The Originality of Lawson*

Indeed, Lawson's stories show no strong resemblance to those of any of his contemporaries. If he seems to us relaxedly at home in the medium, it is because he has refashioned it to suit himself. It is easy for us to underestimate the originality of his architectural achievement, because his designs have been adopted by later builders. In Lawson's time, the short story had not escaped from an essentially narrative purpose—as the novel had, thirty years before. That purpose did not suit Lawson, who wanted not to tell stories for their own sakes but to reveal the Australian way of living and the ethic informing it. Too heavy plotting would have distracted attention from the matter he was expounding, would have dissipated the sense of the simplicity and directness which belonged to the way of life he was revealing. He had to learn how to be successfully "slight," to find just how little plot he could afford to use without risking the collapse of the structure. The bones of episode and development are always there in his more careful work—Lawson did not serve up his slice of life filleted in the modern manner—but they are used only for their right anatomical purpose. It was a delicate problem of craftsmanship which Lawson had to solve, but he handled it at his best with a sure tact.

Thus "That There Dog o' Mine" sets out to celebrate the element of Mateship in the relation between the bushman and his dog. This theme is conveyed by a lengthy speech in which the shearer, Macquarie, describes his companionship with his faithful Tally. A shearer's monologue alone, however, does not make a story, even when it contains all that story's essential communication. So Lawson contrives an element of conflict to introduce the monologue and to carry it structurally. Macquarie has been badly injured in a shanty brawl. Somehow he manages to drag himself ten miles to the nearest hospital. Tally, who has been a "savage but sober participant in the drunken row," and has escaped with a broken leg, limps after him. Macquarie is duly admitted to hospital, but he is informed that Tally must go—dogs are not permitted on the hospital premises. Macquarie promptly staggers toward his swag and prepares to depart: "If you won't take my dog in, you won't take me."

The way is now cleared for the monologue. With its completion the purpose of the story has been achieved; but it cannot end there; the structural element introduced must be completed, and the conflict must be resolved. Since, however, the story's real point is now made, the resolution must be swift without seeming abrupt. Lawson achieves it thus—Macquarie, attempting to depart, collapses and faints:

> Half an hour later, the shearer was comfortably fixed up. "Where's my dog?" he asked, when he came to himself. "Oh, the dog's alright," said the nurse, rather impatiently, "don't bother. The doctor's setting his leg out in the yard." [2]

"Enter Mitchell" (see p. 69) shows how daringly far—considering the literary tenets of the time—Lawson was prepared to go in abandoning plot and risking the accusation of "slightness." Again, though, he does not leave his tiny sketch structureless. Once more a suitably slight element of conflict between swaggie and cabman is introduced and the character delineation subtly twined through it. Again the solution of the conflict is happily achieved, with a touch of surprise, but with no suggestion of mechanical contrivance. Usually, of course, Lawson reared a stronger and longer structure, firming the architectural element to carry a more extended fabric; but, in his best work, it is kept to the minimum necessary for its purpose. It is not permitted to become the center of interest. Thus Lawson anticipated the methods of short story writers of a later generation. It is sometimes assumed that Lawson achieved this original approach by fluke or intuition, or even because he was incapable of solid plotting. Such explanations seem the less likely when one realizes that the contemporary he most resembled in method was Anton Chekov (with whose work, Lawson of course had no acquaintance).

The deliberation of his methods becomes clearer when one observes the supporting skills by which he rendered his structural methods effective. Notice, for instance, the confidence with which he handles the first-person narrative in the *Joe Wilson* stories. He has here set himself a difficult problem, for his selector hero is not the sort of person who can be permitted "to talk like a book." How many later proletarian writers have been wrecked on this reef? Trying to set down the thoughts of their uneducated characters, they have achieved only an irritating syntax and a brittle staccato. Lawson, with no model to help him, strikes the note accurately. The meditations are completely natural, never seeming too articulate for the character, and yet entirely revealing and charged with emotional weight:

"You never saw a child in convulsions? Well, you don't want to. It must be only a matter of seconds, but it seems long minutes; and half an hour afterwards the child might be laughing and playing with you, or stretched out dead. It shook me up a lot. I was always pretty high-strung and sensitive. After Jim took the first fit, every time he cried, or turned over or stretched out in the night, I'd jump. I was always feeling his forehead in the dark to see if he was feverish, or feeling his limbs to see if he was 'limp' yet. Mary and I often laughed about it—afterwards." [3]

It may seem that to render a simple character's speech (or statement of thought) is precisely the kind of achievement which one might expect from a "natural" writer. Such a view would misunderstand the essence of the problem. Even the most naturalistic writer does not set down the words which his character would think or speak. He contrives to produce that illusion while he maintains the superior articulation, precision, and economy of the written language. That speech is right, too, in an element which is one of the most proving evidences of a writer's mastery—the pace. The movement of the passage is very different from the stripped speed aimed at in much post-Hemingway writing, suggesting the beat of trained fingers on typewriter keys. It is equally distant from the unconvincing orotundity of the typical nineteenth-century tale, in which the handler of a quill pen appears to be enjoying the copper-plate elegance of his tracings. Perhaps only an Australian reader can hear the rightness of Joe Wilson's pace; for the bushman developed an unemphatic leisurely rhythm, as distant from the clipped assurance of the upper-class Englishman's speech, as the Texan's drawl is from the Bowery bum's restlessness. Lawson surely suggests the Bushman's relaxed vocal stride.

III *Beginnings and Endings*

One might further test his skill at two points which are usually regarded as crucial to the technical success of a short story, the beginning and the end. In finding how to open a story, Lawson had to abandon the established conventions of his time, which leaned toward a formal and self-conscious beginning—the studied elegance of the elocutionist's bow before he gets to his deadly work. Such a start would have jarred with the simplicity which was essential to Lawson's aim. Set him beside his contemporaries, and the originality of his conception and the smoothness of its execution become almost startlingly apparent. Here is a representative sample of the openings used by Lawson's contemporaries:

> I never pass through Chalk Newton without turning to regard the neighboring upland, at a point where a lane crosses the long straight highway, dividing this from the next parish; a sight which does not fail to recall the event which once happened there . . .

> Once upon a time, very far from England, there lived three men who loved each other so greatly that neither man nor woman could come between them. They were in no sense refined nor to be admitted to the outside-mats of decent folk, because they happened to be

private soldiers in Her Majesty's Army; and private soldiers of our service have small time for self-culture.

Supper was over and there had fallen on the camp the silence that accompanies the rolling of corn-husk cigarettes. The water-hole shone from the dank earth like a patch of fallen sky.

Of all the problems that had been submitted to my friend, Mr. Sherlock Holmes, for solution during our years of intimacy, there were only two that I was the means of introducing to his notice.[4]

And here are the openings of the first three stories in *While the Billy Boils:*

You remember when we hurried home from the old bush school how we were sometimes startled by a bearded apparition, who smiled kindly down on us, and whom our mother introduced, as we raked off our hats, as, "An old mate of your father's on the diggings, Johnny." And he would pat our heads and say we were fine boys, or girls—as the case may have been—and that we had our father's nose but our mother's eyes, or the other way about.

The Western train had just arrived at Redfern station with a lot of ordinary passengers and one swagman. He was short, and stout, and bow-legged, and freckled, and sandy . . .

We were tramping down in Canterbury, Maoriland, at the time, swagging it—me and Bill—looking for work on the new railway-line. Well, one afternoon, after a long hot tramp, we comes to Stiffner's Hotel—between Christchurch and that other place—I forget the name of it—with throats on us like sunstroke bones, and not the price of a stick of tobacco.

That easy, natural slide into the story is, to modern ears at least, a great improvement on the stiff gesturing of Lawson's contemporaries. It may be supposed that it is simply the triumph of the natural writer over the self-conscious. Such a view would show little appreciation of the difficulties of simplicity. Again it is with the closely deliberated methods of Chekov that Lawson shows the closest correspondence, as a random selection of the Russian writer's openings may suggest:

> Ivan Alexiyitch Ognev remembers how on that August evening he opened the glass door with a rattle and went out on to the verandah. He was wearing . . .

> One day when she was younger and better-looking, and when her voice was stronger, Nikolay Petrovitch Kolpakov, her adorer, was sitting in the outer room in her summer villa.

> The Superintendent said to me "I only keep you out of regard for your worthy father; but for that you would have been sent flying long ago." I replied to him, "You flatter me too much in supposing that I am capable of flying." [5]

In his handling of the endings of his stories, Lawson showed an even deeper artistry. Again his aim raised for him difficult problems. The elegantly rounded-off close would not have suited the simplicity of his atmosphere. On the other hand, the snap finish, the last triumphant clap of the hammer on the nail driven home, would not have done either. Lawson's aim was not to tell a tale but to evoke the quality of Australian living; and the evocative tale must end not with a bang but an echo. The stone having plunged in the pool, the ripples must widen out, to vanish in mystery. Lawson is a master of this final reverberation. His stories seldom end at the point which the merely narrative interest suggests. Any student of the craft of fiction could learn much by looking for the point where he would have been tempted to end a Lawson story, and observing how, with a further touch, Lawson prolongs the overtones. Let him beware of imitation, though, for unless the echo contains the inimitable touch of humane wisdom, the mechanical device will not become the mode of an artist.

Let me emphasize the point by challenging the reader's ingenuity. I have already outlined the story of "Telling Mrs. Baker" (see p. 67). The narrative ends with the incident of the nice city girl kissing the two bushmen. The final sentences of the paragraph describing the incident read: "I was taller than Andy and had to stoop. 'Goodbye,' she said and ran to the gate and in, waving her hand to us. We lifted our hats again and turned down the road." This is the right final episode for a story which is essentially an evocation of sentiment, and it would have been tempting to make it the actual ending of the tale, but it would not have worked well.

If the reader's after-feeling is left to run on from here, the effect of the sentiment may degenerate into sentimentality. Something more must be done to hedge the story against this danger, but no new action can be introduced at this stage. Well, try it for yourself. How would you balance the effect, without introducing new material? It isn't easy, is it? Yet how easy Lawson makes it look. He adds ten words: "I don't think it did either of us any harm" [6] and the balance of tone is precisely achieved.

IV *Balance Through Irony*

His escape, in the best stories of his best period, from the collapse of sentiment into sentimentality is due primarily to the steadiness of his vision; but it is helped by two consciously used devices, neither of them of a kind that we expect from a natural writer: effective understatement and the ironic twist at the danger point. The first adds weight to the feeling as well as a saving moderation. In "Middleton's Peter," for example, Lawson concludes by describing the death of Doc Wilde and suggesting the strong feeling which the bush-folk had for that mately cynic. To have written, as an average nineteenth-century tale-spinner might, "They kept his memory ever-green, in their hearts," would have been weak as well as cloying. To say, as Lawson does, "they buried him with bush-honours and chiselled his name on a slab of blue-gum—a wood that lasts" [7] suggests the strong tug of undercurrents.

It takes an even finer artistry to use irony as an antiseptic at the moment of danger, as Lawson often did. Thus "Mitchell on Matrimony" discourses of the little things that men ought to do for their wives, and don't. It is truthful observation (or experience), it is sincerely felt, and it is moving; but it is also highly sentimental—the taste is a little too sweet; so Lawson contrives an ironic touch to cleanse the reader's palate with its tartness. Having digested Mitchell's sermon on the importance of husbandly consideration, his mate voices a not unnatural curiosity:

"How is your wife now, Mitchell?"
"I don't know," said Mitchell calmly.
"Don't know?" echoed the mate. "Didn't you treat her well?"
"Ah, well, I tried to."
"Well, did you put your theory into practice?"

"I did," said Mitchell, very deliberately.

Joe waited, but nothing came.

"Well?" he asked impatiently. "How did it act? Did it work well?"

"I don't know," said Mitchell (puff); "she left me."

"What!"

Mitchell jerked the half-smoked pipe from his mouth, and rapped the burning tobacco out against the toe of his boot.

"She left me," he said, standing up and stretching himself. Then, with a vicious jerk of the arm, "She left me for—another kind of fellow!"

He looked east towards the public-house, where they were taking the coach-horses from the stable.

"Why don't you finish your tea, Joe? The billy's getting cold." [8]

If the incident on which Lawson had based "Shooting the Moon" had fallen into the hands of the ordinary yarn-spinner, it would have been no more than a piece of flat bush-farce. Observe how Lawson, refusing three possible ending points, weaves together strands of irony, homely humor, sentiment, and the beautifully judged prolonging echo. Mitchell is describing a moonlight flit from a pub:

Well, Tom agreed to go, and presently I saw a shadow under the window and lowered away.

"All right?" I asked in a whisper.

"All right!" whispered the shadow. I lowered the other swag.

"All right?"

"All right," said the shadow, and just then the moon came out. But it wasn't all right. It was the landlord himself!

It seems he got up and went out to the back in the night, and just happened to be coming in when my mate Tom was sneaking out of the back door. He saw Tom, and Tom saw him, and smoked through a hole in the palings into the scrub. The boss looked up at the window, and dropped to it. I went down, funky enough, I can tell you, and faced him. He said:

"Look here, mate, why didn't you come straight to me, and tell me how you were fixed, instead of sneaking round the trouble in that fashion? There's no occasion for it."

I felt mean at once, but I said, "Well, you see, we didn't know you, boss."

"So it seems. Well, I didn't think of that. Anyway, call up your mate and come and have a drink; we'll talk over it afterwards." So I called Tom. "Come on," I shouted, "it's all right."

"And the boss kept us a couple of days, and then gave us as much tucker as we could carry, and a drop of stuff and a few bob to go on the track again with."

"Well, he was white, any road."

"Yes, I knew him well after that, and only heard one man say a word against him."

"And did you stoush him?"

"No. I was going to, but Tom wouldn't let me. He said he was frightened I might make a mess of it, and he did it himself."

"Did what? Make a mess of it?"

"He made a mess of the other man that slandered the publican. I'd be funny if I was you. Where's the matches?"

"And could Tom fight?"

"Yes. Tom could fight."

"Did you travel long with him after that?"

"Ten years."

"And where is he now?"

"Dead—Give us the matches." [9]

V *Influence of the Campfire Yarn*

Mention of these two stories suggests a possible source of Lawson's technical know-how. Like most men living remote from sophisticated forms of entertainment, the bushmen practiced the art of yarn-spinning. Drovers taking cattle or sheep to the railheads, the bullock-drivers whose wagons carried supplies to the outback stations, sundowners tramping the roads in search of work or its skilful avoidance, came together at convenient camping places beside a stream. Here the bush-ritual of "boiling the billy" would be discharged, a meal would be prepared over the open fire, and the chance-assembled gathering would then suck at their pipes and exchange yarns. Many of the practitioners of this do-it-yourself entertainment acquired considerable skill in their art. Lawson must often have been an auditor at such performances, particularly during the months of his wanderings "back o' Bourke." One can imagine him battling against his deafness in his eagerness to harvest securely this manna of "copy."

It is impossible to know how much of his skill he learned from such masters. Certainly he made shrewd use of the setting of the camp-fire yarn. The device of reported narrative was, of course, a popular story form of his day, and was usually a painfully boring convention. You know the sort of thing:

"That reminds me," said Patrick Lorimer, kicking absently at the coals of the blazing fire, "of an incident which happened on my last big game-hunting expedition to Lobingula."

There were six of us sipping our whisky at St. Gideon's Hall, all men of wide experience.

Then the story is launched, and no more is heard of the narrator or St. Gideon's until the perfunctory winding up, which usually weakens the impact of the real story. The device is no more than a piece of machinery which distracts us by its preliminary whirr and its final hiccough. But with Lawson, the narrator remains a prime character in the story—particularly if he is Mitchell—adding perspective to the narration; the setting of the story's telling is kept discreetly alive for us by reminders spaced through the tale with a nice judgment. More than that, the interchange between the narrator and his audience adds extra significance, softening or rounding the tone and prolonging the echo. The two stories which I have just quoted illustrate Lawson's use of this device.

VI *Lawson's Development*

Further evidence of the deliberation of Lawson's methods is provided by the development of his technique. He came to mastery with astonishing swiftness. Many of the stories in *While the Billy Boils*, his first professionally published volume, have a confidence, an originality, and a delicacy of touch which suggest a succession of wastepaper baskets filled with preliminary failures, rather than the work of the hard-pressed, uneducated freelance struggling to establish himself.

His second volume, *On the Track and Over the Sliprail*, published four years later, is disappointing. Professor Colin Roderick's selection of twenty Lawson stories[10] contains ten from the first volume, only four from the second. I am not in full agreement with the methods of Professor Roderick's selection, but I believe that this proportion fairly indicates the comparative merits of the two volumes. There is a disconcerting retreat toward the conventional in the second of them. In particular, several of the longer stories are plot-centered in the accepted manner of the time. This is particularly noticeable in "The Hero of Redclay," the narrative Lawson had originally intended to develop into a novel, if we may accept a publisher's notice in the reprint of *While the Billy Boils*. I have a hunch (unsupported by any scrap of evidence) that Archibald was discussing this or a story of similar mold when he made a remark which Lawson has recorded:

> He'd often say to a young writer whose style was changing—or who was trying new lines: "Yes, the sketch" (or whatever it was) "is very good, but it isn't *you* somehow. Why don't you lay to your book? This is out of your line." [11]

Certainly, these heavily plotted stories are not in Lawson's line. Their attempted dramatizations do not give his delicacy a chance to make its effect.

The next volume, *Joe Wilson and His Mates,* came out a year later and shows not merely a return to form but an expansion of Lawson's technical resources. Examining it, one realizes the explanation of the aberrations in *On the Track and Over the Sliprail.* Lawson is searching for a more extended form. First he had nourished the idea of writing a novel. Either he could not command enough steady writing time to achieve this intention or he belatedly realized that it was not his "line." Then he attempted the longer plot-centered stories which make heavy weather of his second collection. Perhaps Lawson was trying to silence those conventional critics who found his work too "slight."

In the stories of the *Joe Wilson* volume, Lawson has solved his problem. He here often expands the scope of his narrative, giving himself room for fuller explorations. To prevent this more extended material from sagging, he buttresses it with mildly dramatic episodes; but he does not make the mistake of centering the interest in these episodes rather than in the human figures whom he is presenting. The supporting episode reveals the nature of those figures, but it is what they are, rather than what they do, that matters. "Telling Mrs. Baker" and "A Hero in Dingo Scrubs" are good examples of this method successfully employed. A variant approach can be observed in "The Babies in the Bush." Here Lawson holds his comparatively lengthy structure firm first by introducing us to an enigmatic figure and then by gradually unrolling the past circumstances which explain the enigma.

VII *The* Joe Wilson *Stories*

The most interesting, and the most successful, experiment in fuller deployment is to be found in the first four stories of the volume, constituting a separate section called "Joe Wilson." These four connected tales are first-person narrations by Joe Wilson, which leisurely describe his engagement and the early years of his marriage. They constitute, in my opinion, the finest of Lawson's achievements.

Lawson later returned to this device of the connected series of stories in *Triangles of Life*. The structural design here is both more ambitious and subtler; but the series belongs to the years of Lawson's decline, when he could no longer breathe convincing life into his conceptions. Nevertheless, I believe he was right in the conviction which presumably underlay this return to the structural method of Joe Wilson—the conviction that the device of the connected series of stories happily suited him. It gives him room for freer movement and for deeper penetrations without imposing the weight of plotting and the need for the overtly dramatic which, when he attempted them, seemed to crush his delicacy flat.

Certainly the plot element in "Joe Wilson" is remarkably slight to sustain a narrative of well over 40,000 words. The first story, "Joe Wilson's Courtship," simply narrates the falling-in-love of a naïve and blundering youth. It ambles along with a dryly observant eye for the humors of its well-worn theme; but, with an angler's shrewdness, Lawson recognizes the moment when the line must be tautened if the reader's interest is to be kept on the hook. At this point he stiffens the structure with the incident of Joe's fight with an unpleasant fellow who has spoken slightingly of the girl. Even here, however, there is no real straying of interest from character to mere incident. The emphasis is kept on the psychological reaction of Joe Wilson (alias Henry Lawson), his distaste for the brutality of fisticuffs overborne by the idealism which demands that an insulted beloved must be avenged. He wins his fight, of course, as a hero should; but characteristically Lawson depicts the incident with a domestic naturalness. There are no storybook heroics; yet Lawson convincingly suggests the triumph of an honest simplicity. This incident leads, with an easy logic, to the accepted proposal which concludes the courtship.

In the next story, "Brighten's Sister-in-law," we find the couple married, with a child of three, struggling to establish themselves on a selection. Joe goes to the nearest township to collect Jim—the child—who has been staying with relatives. When the two camp for the night on the way home, Jim displays the preliminary symptoms of an attack of convulsions, to which he is subject. Joe is desperate; the nearest doctor is fifteen miles away. Then he seems to see in the sky a vision of a woman pointing in a certain direction, and he remembers that five miles off in that direction is the homestead of the Brightens. Not that they are likely to be of much use, for they are a hopelessly derelict couple. But Joe also remembers that Mrs. Brighten's sister, a trained nurse, is staying with them. He mounts his horse with the child held across the saddle and gallops wildly for the Brighten's hut. There the nurse takes charge and saves the child.

The remainder of the story is mainly taken up with a character study of this woman. She has the tough-seeming harshness which nurses often use to safeguard their professional competence; but Lawson implies, by a series of touches, that in her case it guards from soft betrayal the frustration of her maternal instinct. The tailpiece to the story takes us back to the theme of Mary and Joe's relationship. It is a characteristic passage in which Lawson walks the edge of the precipice bordering sentimentality, which the writer proclaiming the values of sentiment must tread:

> Nothing would suit Mary but she must go over to Brighten's shanty and see Brighten's sister-in-law. So James drove her over one morning in the spring-cart: it was a long way, and they stayed at Brighten's overnight and didn't get back till late the next afternoon. I'd got the place in a pig-muck, as Mary said, "doing for" myself, and I was having a snooze on the sofa when she got back. The first thing I remember was someone stroking my head and kissing me, and I heard Mary saying "My poor boy!"
>
> I sat up with a jerk. I thought Jim had gone off again. But it seems that Mary was only referring to me. Then she started to pull grey hairs out of my head and put them in a match-box—to see how many she'd get. She used to do this when she felt a bit soft.[12]

Some readers may reject my evaluation of this passage; they may feel that it is soft and sentimentalized, a concession to those readers who prefer the comforting to the confrontation of truth. I do not agree. In its context it seems to me to convey, with an admirably evocative reticence, the influence of shared pain in creating the relationship which is marriage.

One cannot find any such defense for another incident in the story. The reader's eyebrows may already have shot up at my reference to the supernatural vision which pointed Joe to the Brighten's hut. He may have wondered how such a touch could be reconciled with that fidelity to life-as-it-is to which, I have suggested, Lawson adhered. It cannot be so reconciled; it sticks out as incongruously as a conventionally executed gargoyle jammed on a functionally designed cottage. It seems to suggest in Lawson a streak of cheap opportunism. The true explanation, as I believe, is of some interest to students of the literary process.

Lawson often earned himself two checks for one idea by using it in both a story and a set of verses. The idea of "Brighten's Sister-in-law" reappears in a poem called "The Old Head Nurse." The second version almost certainly records the actual incident on which the idea was based. Lawson's son Jim was taken with convulsions in their Sydney home. During a temporary respite in the struggle to save the child's life Lawson wandered to the street door, for no reason which he could afterward explain. At that moment the nurse who had been in charge of a ward in which he had been a patient came down the street, "Having a holiday—first in her life—and resting, of course, on her restless feet." [13] Lawson appealed for her help; she took charge of the situation and saved the child. A man as emotional and as simple-natured as Lawson could hardly dismiss the incident as mere coincidence; to him it must have seemed an intervention of providence. When, therefore, he used the story in "Joe Wilson," he felt impelled to include the suggestion of a parallel providential intervention recasting the details (not very happily) to fit the changed setting and circumstances of the *Joe Wilson* story. It is not the only occasion in literary history when a writer has been betrayed into unconvincingness by the insistent need to include that which actually happened, or the nearest approach to it which his framework would enclose.

The following story, "Water Them Geraniums," seems, to a superficial view, irrelevant. It is concerned mainly with Mrs. Spicer, neighbor to the Wilsons, occupying a farm even more wretched than theirs. This is the most detailed of all Lawson's studies of the "haggard women," and it is one of the most moving. Mrs. Spicer has had most of the vitality ground out of her by the pressures and the loneliness of her life, but she maintains a determined resistance to circumstance and clings desperately to such remnants of "respectable" living as she can muster. The story ends with her appallingly lonely death.

This may seem to have little to do with the history of the Wilsons; but that would be a myopic view. The story is introduced by an account of a quarrel between Mary and Joe—a classic little incident in which the tone and method of a matrimonial row are precisely suggested. Mary is most irritatingly wrong in the logic of her arguments, most damningly right in the emotional bases underlying her anger at Joe. That anger is sparked by the sinking of the heart with which Mary observes the uncivilized bleakness of the new home at which she has just arrived, the faltering of her courage as she realizes the desperation of the struggle which lies before the couple. A few hours later she has recovered her usual cheerful resolution, but the "making-up" kiss is incompletely successful because Mary's mouth is filled with tacks. This characteristically domestic touch accurately symbolizes a feeling of incompleteness in the reconciliation, a recognition that Mary has fought down her forebodings but has not destroyed them.

With this introduction, the figure of Mrs. Spicer acquires a special significance. She hangs over Mary like a cloud, threatening the happy young wife with the spiritual erosions which have almost destroyed the older woman leading the kind of life which Mary must face. Lawson is too shrewd a writer to declare this meaning flatly. He adds an oblique suggestion conveyed in a snatch of dialogue:

"Well-no, Mrs. Wilson," she said in a groping sort of voice, "I uster once. . . . I somehow seem to have got past carin'. Besides—besides Spicer was a very different man then to what he is now. He's got so moody and gloomy at home he hardly ever speaks."

Mary sat silent for a minute thinking. Then Mrs. Spicer roused herself:

"Oh, I don't know what I'm talking about! You mustn't take any notice of me, Mrs. Wilson—I don't often go on like this. I do believe I'm gettin' a bit ratty at times. It must be the heat and the dullness. . . ."

I walked home with her a piece along the creek. She said nothing for a long time, and seemed to be thinking in a puzzled way. Then she said suddenly: "What-did-you-bring-her-here-for? She's only a girl." [14]

It is enough; only the least imaginative reader could now fail to sense the menace of Mrs. Spicer's fate threatening the fresh and lovable personality of Mary Wilson.

In the final story, "A Double-Buggy at Lahey's Creek," the atmosphere lightens, although Lawson modulates gradually into the new key. The Wilsons have a good season; timely rain combines with a successful initiative of Mary's to give the couple a good return. At last Joe has a little money in his pocket, and at last he can give Mary the status symbol for which she hankers—a double-buggy. Most of the story is taken up with the details of the purchase, with the interest of the folk in the township who add subsidiary gifts to grace the triumph—gifts which convey their sympathy with the simple-hearted integrity of this struggling couple —and with the homecoming, ingeniously contrived to give the maximum surprise to Mary. The final picture which the story leaves with the reader is that of Mary and Joe sitting in their buggy in the stable: ". . . we hadn't had such a comfortable seat for years"—and then embarrassedly climbing down lest some passer-by should see them, ". . . for we began to feel like a pair of fools up there." [15]

Such an outline of the material of the *Joe Wilson* stories can convey only one point: the slenderness of the basis on which Lawson has reared his most sustained achievement. There is, indeed, a certain slightness in the achievement in itself. It has no largeness of power; it does not explore spiritual deeps or sweep us away on ocean tides of emotion. Its analysis of the nature of marriage is admirably truthful as far as it goes, but it leaves out much. It sees the relationship merely as a special form of Mateship. Its triumphs are only those of tenderness; there is no attempt to suggest the spiritual emancipations or the psychological complexities of sexual love. Such triumphs were beyond Lawson's range; he could no more attempt them than Jane Austen could. But within its limitations the story series moves us and charms us in a way that a summary of its content cannot begin to suggest. It is a miniature, but it is a miniature achieved with a humane and confident artistry, apart from one or two touches of sentiment which are a little too syrupy (notably, unhappily, in the first page of the first story).

The development of Lawson's art shown in this series is not merely in the conquest of his main technical problem: how to fill a larger canvas with the light-flicking brushstrokes through which his artistry most effectively worked. He has also crossed a line of great importance in the development of any writer. Hitherto he has been essentially an observer. He sees a man or woman and reports his or her condition, although, of course, both his selections and his treatment reveal the subconscious direction of his approach to life. Now he is not just reporting lives—an individual view of the nature of life gets itself declared.

That view of Life may be roughly epitomized as an almost desperately gloomy interpretation of the human situation redeemed by "the insecurely triumphant survival of tenderness through endurance." These stories are suffused with Lawson's melancholy. That may seem a curious declaration to make about a work which begins with the picture of an innocent wooing and ends with the achievement of the double-buggy. The melancholy is obliquely suggested. A reader who had completed the book would certainly be aware of its presence, but he might have difficulty in specifying the passages from which it arose.

I have already indicated how Lawson uses the figure of Mrs. Spicer to cast a shadow on Mary Wilson. Although Lawson makes this point with a discreet indirection, it is a far more obvious assertion of the melancholy interpretation of life than most of the touches which he uses for that purpose. I can perhaps best indicate their nature by reference to the coda of the first story. The last narrative-detail of that story is Mary's acceptance of her lover. Lawson rounds the incident off with a neat touch which might effectively have served as the final lines of the story:

> "Why won't you kiss me, Mary? Don't you love me?"
> "Because," she said, "because—because I—I don't—I don't think it right for a girl to—to kiss a man unless she's going to be his wife."
> Then it dawned on me! I'd forgot all about proposing.
> "Mary," I said, "would you marry a chap like me?"
> And that was all right.

Lawson, however, does not end here. Mary's guardian is that squatter Black who has married an English wife "who never got any Australian notions." Mary insists that Joe must apply to Black for permission to marry her. Joe finds him sitting on a log talking to an old bushman. Shortly, Joe takes the bushman's place. Black makes a little desultory conversation, including that "bitter" remark about "Mrs. Black running the station now," which apprises the reader of the unsatisfactory state of the squatter's marriage. Joe eventually gets out his request:

> He puffed at his pipe for a long time, then I thought he spoke.
> "What did you say, boss?" I said.
> "Nothing, Joe," he said, "I was going to say a lot, but it wouldn't be any use. My father used to say a lot to me before I was married."
> I waited a good while for him to speak.
> "Well, boss," I said, "What about Mary?"
> "Oh! I suppose that's all right, Joe," he said. "I-I beg your pardon. I got thinking of the days when I was courting Mrs. Black." [16]

It is an admirable touch. The story has hitherto held the bright colorings of young love. The tailpiece casts a shadow over the coloring, suggesting the insecurity of the couple's happiness. A series of such touches continues to suggest the melancholy element in the interpretation of the nature of marriage, which is the theme of the stories. That influence is largely dissipated, of course, in the last story, for here Lawson is declaring the reconciling element, the survival of tenderness. The meaning of the work might be thus roughly epitomized: "Life is a painful business. Marriage, even with love, is a difficult relationship. But there is an insecure triumph when a Joe Wilson buys his wife a double-buggy." How hopelessly inadequate that must sound. The purchase of a double-buggy must seem absurdly trivial, tepidly sentimentalized, as a symbol of Lawson's reconciling conviction. But how right Lawson's treatment makes it. It does, in effect, precisely declare the nature of the triumphant survival of tenderness; at the same time, it keeps the treatment within that scale of life-as-it-is which is necessary to Lawson's achievement. Moreover it helps him to escape the truthless comforting wishful thinking of the conventional happy ending. We are moved by the incident and we are charmed by it, but we are in no danger of mistaking it for finality. The triumphant survival of tenderness has the right measure of insecurity.

I have already mentioned one limitation on Lawson's success in these stories which was probably inherent in his nature: his inability to deal with passion or to suggest strength. One cannot imagine that he would ever have escaped from this weakness. There is a second limitation in these stories which he seems to be in process of overcoming. He had crossed the line which divides observation of living from interpretation of life. But his conception of Life was not yet fully developed. It was still tangled with the acceptance of conventional views which could not be assimilated to his individual intuitions. He had not yet full confidence in his melancholy. He seemed to need another ten years to build his experience into coherent concepts, to strain out of them the alloy of borrowed assumptions. At the same time he has plainly made an exciting beginning on this process. To an informed reader of the time, he must have seemed a writer to watch with alert expectancy. There are signs that Lawson himself knew this, that his ambitions at this time were widening, his confidence in his own powers strengthening.

In fact, of course, the development never took place. The transplantation to England disturbed his concentration on the creative process; the death of Hannah crushed it. It is a disappointment which is unusually hard to take. One can accept the early death of an Emily Brontë or a John Keats, despite one's sense of what those deaths cost us, for death at least has dignity; but the living collapse of a talent which seemed about to add depth to its already achieved sureness and originality—this is almost unendurable.

VIII *Lawson's Verse*

There remains the ungrateful task of saying something about Lawson's verse. In truth, there is little to be said about it, or for it. It is pretty much the same as that produced by the reasonably competent among the bush-balladists who abounded in Australia at the time. Lawson's fine gift for observation, his selective sureness of touch in conveying it, still often worked within the verse form, though the kind of themes which Lawson attempted in his verse less often called it into play. I have said that in his literary punchup with Paterson, Lawson wrote the better of the two; but here the nature of the debate forced them to play the engagement on Lawson's home ground of observant description. Elsewhere

Paterson is the better ballad-writer. He can produce the strong flow of simple narrative which best suits the form and which gives no space for the subtler gifts of Lawson. Even when, in a Lawson ballad, a reader enjoys some happy touch of observation, some humane and perceptive warmth of interpretation, that reader is still likely to regret that Lawson did not use prose. Sometimes the constrictive demands of rhythm and rhyme force his choice of a phrase, and he is unable to balance the loss by an effective use of the musical evocations achieved by the poet of vocation. He falls into the imposed conventional lollop of the line, which only the finest ballad-writers can escape.

The cultural immaturity of the Australian society of the time made the ballad a natural form for its attempts at artistic self-expression. That predominance tempted Lawson into the use of a method which did not suit him. A further immaturity in the community created a more dangerous temptation. This artistically naïve people did not draw the necessary distinction between "poetry" and "verse." A metrist was for them a poet, even a Poet. They therefore often accorded to the balladist the high, magical status which almost all communities before the present epoch have bestowed upon the poet as the successor to the seer. There are indications that Lawson sometimes accepted this indiscriminate assumption: that he was able to convince himself that he became a seer by the mere process of expressing warm emotional responses in verse, without practicing those imaginative disciplines which can alone justify the assumption.

The hypnotic effect of rhythm seems often to have lulled his judgment to sleep. The perceptive wariness, which protected this man of sentiment from collapsing into sentimentality, vanished when that hypnosis worked upon him. In his verse he often wallows in third-rate sentimentalized conceptions like a tired man relaxing in a tepid bath.

The difference is often startingly obvious, when the prose and verse expressions of a similar idea are set together. Thus, Lawson uses the legend of the bush-fairies who look after lost children in a ballad as well as in the story "The Babies in the Bush" (see p. 91). In the verses it is the central theme of the work, which thus becomes as nauseatingly syrupy a piece of sentimentalizing as one would expect.[17] When Lawson has the idea of using the legend in a story, his now alert judgment warns him that it won't do as the central theme. It therefore becomes the delusion of the demented mother. Thus used, it effectively suggests her self-protective retreat into immaturity of mind. More than that, the innocence of the idea increases our sympathy with the destroyed woman, while its fatuity, on the rational level of judgment, increases our sense of the pain which the guilty husband must endure. The idea which led to a sticky pathos in the verses produces a creative imaginative effect in the prose version.

This difference of level between the best of Lawson's prose and almost all of his verse is a strange phenomenon, intriguing to the literary student. It is not, of course, unusual for a writer to handle prose well and verse mediocrely. The intriguing point is that the imaginative conceptions, the artistic judgment, should work on such different levels in the two forms. No reader could doubt that Lawson's ultimate success rests on his humane warmth, his sympathetic perception, and the precise play of his observation. His mastery of prose craftsmanship is only the process through which these qualities declare themselves. And yet, in the verse form where his technical mastery no longer works, he also often loses these imaginative gifts. It is an unexpected result which suggests that the psychological connection between the mechanics of writing and the processes of imaginative creation is far more involved than is generally assumed.

CHAPTER 6

Critical Roundabout

IN THE critical discussions of such a writer as Lawson, one expects to find two streams of opinion, complementary in their judgments, the one emanating from his popular audience, the other expressing the more precise and objective valuations of the professional litterateurs and the cultivated dillettanti. In practice, however, it was forty years after Lawson's emergence as a writer before the second kind of voice became clearly audible in Australia. In the nineties and the ensuing decades, Australian academics and the middle-class people of culture were, with a few exceptions, disdainful of Australian writing. Such stuff was mainly associated with the Sydney *Bulletin,* and that paper was anathema to most respectable bourgeois. It encouraged the absurd demands of the working classes; it was written in a deplorably slangy style; and it showed disrespect for the royal family. The respectable could hardly admit that the writers whom it nurtured had anything to do with the grand rituals of literature.[1]

Consequently, until about 1930, judgments of Lawson came mainly from his bushman-like admirers. There are not a great many such judgments, for the early lovers of Lawson were not the kind of people to rush into print; nor are those eulogies which did appear very enlightening, for those who wrote them did not have either the training or the inclination for scholarly precision. They preferred to convey the warmth of their affection in a prose freely sprinkled with rhetorical abstraction.

Certain general tendencies can, however, be discerned in these writings, which often have the charm of an honest warmth of feeling. One is a general inclination to regard Lawson as essentially a poet—without drawing pettifogging, highbrow distinctions between balladry and the higher forms of the poetic art. These admirers by no means despised Lawson's stories, but they plainly regarded them as subsidiary to his main achievement. The other is a tendency to assume that Lawson was a "natural"—almost a Grandma Moses of writing—who did not worry about technique and who triumphed over a lack of "book-learning" and a personal indifference to artistic knowhow. One gathers that his admirers rather preferred it that way. The word "artistry" perhaps suggested, for them, an arrogant distance from ordinary humanity.

The first assumption is clearly observable in a lecture delivered by J. M. Neild. Its date is 1944, but Neild was then an old man, and his attitude is typical of an earlier generation, although that attitude still tenuously exists and is sometimes aired at gatherings of the Henry Lawson Societies, which were founded in Melbourne and Sydney a few years after Lawson's death. Professor Joseph Jones, attending such a gathering in 1961, observed "a cumulative mystique about the proceedings which overlapped into the religious." [2] Neild was a versifier who began to write about the same time as Lawson. He achieved some notoriety as the author of the superb line "Eftsoons the nocent waterspout will rise." [3] His lecture gives by far the strongest emphasis to Lawson's poetry. The first two pages are sprinkled with such phrases as "immortal poet-laureate . . . wonderful minstrelsy . . . poet's outpourings . . . national singer . . . soul of poetry . . . native singer . . . great Australian poet fit to rank with the immortals."[4] No comparable burst of epithets marks Neild's treatment of Lawson's prose.

The same emphasis appears in a series of lectures on Australian literature delivered by Mrs. Zora Cross at the Sydney Teachers' College in 1922: "Though his prose is the more bulky part of his work, I think it is of less importance than his verse; but that may be because of the early influence of those old mates of my childhood." [5] The personal reason there adduced goes far to explain—and partly to justify—the early popular preference for Lawson's verse. Earlier in her lecture, Mrs. Cross described how, as a child in a country home, she would sneak out to the camps of wayfarers to listen to the evening's entertainment there provided. The amateur buskers of the group would sing or recite Australian folk songs or ballads. Soon one of the audience would say "Give us one of Harry's, Andy" and the bush-elocutionist would oblige with a Lawson ballad.[6]

Reading that passage, and envying Mrs. Cross her experience, I feel some qualms over my unenthusiastic judgment of Lawson's balladry. I do not retract that judgment, but I find a certain stiffness of attitude in it. It does not take enough account of the needs of those evenings of popular national song in the men's quarters during the nineties, and later. They were important evenings; indeed, their influence remains important for the Australians of today. They helped to create an Australian individuality, to lay a foundation on which the nation could develop toward cultural maturity. That child crouched in the shadows near the log fire, drinking in the "bits of Harry" in the conditions which gave them most meaning—surely she was acquiring a "humane education" in the fullest meaning of the term.

It may be objected that Lawson's stories were not only of finer quality than his verse, but that they were equally accessible by the popular mind. They suffered, however, from two defects for the particular purpose which I have been discussing. Lawson seldom used prose to declare the revolutionary political creed of his early years, and that element was important in his influence. In prose, he was not "hot-hearted Henry Lawson" as a brother radical poet has described him.[7] Moreover, a Lawson story would be difficult to memorize and harder to render as an effective recitation. It could not be effectively used as part of the campfire evening ritual.

The assumption that Lawson was a "natural" writer, unconcerned with technical niceties, was perhaps best expressed by Arthur Bayldon. He is hardly typical of the bushman enthusiasts. He was an Englishman who migrated to Australia in 1891, when he was twenty-six, and he had already published volumes of verse before he left England. Nevertheless, he was expressing the popular view, though he shaped it with some sophistication, when he wrote:

> A highly emotional temperament, with quick objective perception and an excellent memory, are his literary make-up, supplemented by grim humour at times and a laudable desire to stick to facts—scouting everything invented, the trickery of plots, the artificiality of preconceived literary effects, as little less than a crime. So long as his stories contain his conceptions—the emotions, the feelings that possessed him—he troubles little how these have been presented. Bret Harte had a literary facility and a theatrical dexterity beyond Lawson who probably does not desire them.[8]

There is a measure of essential truth in this judgment, but it does much less than justice to the shrewdness and the purposive shaping which directed Lawson's technique.

The same attitude can be observed in the comments in Professor E. Morris Miller's *Bibliography of Australian Literature*. Miller's professorial rank may suggest to the reader that he must represent an academic rather than a popular view. Miller, however, held a chair of philosophy, and he did not lay claim to literary erudition. He came to the task of completing an Australian bibliography and providing its critical comments largely because no better equipped scholar seemed likely to undertake it. His mind had more in common with the popular Australian reader than with the professional scholar of literature.

His view of Lawson's technique is summed up in the phrase "he wrote artlessly" [9]—a word which recurs strangely often in discussions of Lawson. His general discussion conveys the idea that there is little shaping in Lawson's work, and that he succeeds by virtue of the truth of his perception, presented with a fitting ingenuousness.

I *The Enthusiasts and Lawson's Decline*

The early drying up of Lawson's gift and the long period of his decline could not be ignored by the enthusiasts who had set him up as the unrivaled literary exponent of emergent Australianism; but his failure did not unseat him from his eminence. His admirers accepted it philosophically, perhaps believing that defeat by alcoholism was the occupational hazard of writers. They were less ready to accept the increasingly lugubrious tone of his work. There had always been a measure of resistance to the melancholy in Lawson's writing—as Paterson's gibe at "the graveyard poet" suggests (see p. 90). That flavor did not fit well with the ebullience of Australian nationalistic fervor. The bushmen accepted it with only occasional restiveness because it was part of their Harry's makeup and had to be taken along with the revolutionary fire, the championship of the underdog, the warmth of sympathy, and the strength of admiration for bushman character which had won their love for their poet.

But in the years of his decline, Lawson's melancholy acquired a morbid tone of self-pity. He sounded like a whiner, and that could not be accepted. A bushman might call his mate "an old bastard," implying only affection, decently free from too naked an emotionalism; but if a bushman called his friend a whiner, he was looking for fight or the dissolution of mateship.

Even such close friends of Lawson as Le Gay Brereton or E. J. Brady assailed him in print for the gloom of his later verses. The balladist "Gilrooney" (R. J. Casey) adjured him in the pages of the *Bulletin* to:

> Give verse a mirthful setting
> Away from vain regretting
> And you shall still be King.[10]

"D. M. W." (David McKee Wright) was more pretentiously admonitory along the same rather fatuous lines:

> This is a lay of Henry Lawson and a Lay of What-the-Devil's-Gone-Wrong?
> It is also a poem of Lost Endeavour and an ode of Lift-Up-Your-Head-and-Shine.
> But, first and chief, it's the lyrical statement of Damn-it-Get-Singing-and-Cease-to-Pine.
> It is also a poem of Make-us-Remember, and a truthful song of We-Can't-Forget,
> And a prophecy he can fulfill if he wants to do. He'll sing the Song of Australia yet.[11]

Reading "D. M. W.'s" ballad, I found this patronizing note from so vapid a versifier a little hard to take; but my distaste stiffened a good deal when I realized the circumstances behind its composition. Leafing back through the *Bulletin* in search of the contribution by Lawson which Wright was answering, I found that it was "The Song of Prison." [12] The contents of that ballad leave no doubt that it was written in Darlinghurst Jail.

II *A. G. Stephens*

In the absence of considered comment on Lawson's work from academic sources and from literary journals, A. G. Stephens comes nearest to expressing contemporary reaction by cultured Australians to the popular favorite. In some ways he is hardly a typical representative of educated middle-class opinion. He was mainly a self-educated man; but he had done the job well, and could confidently have kept up his end in a literary conversation with an Oxbridge honors graduate, provided the Englishman did not cheat by quoting Greek.

Stephens was the son of the editor of a country paper and was early apprenticed to his father's trade. He joined the *Bulletin* staff in his mid-twenties, and by 1896 he had created for himself the post of Literary Editor. There are some signs that Stephens did not fully share the paper's Radical outlook, but he was certainly in full sympathy with its Australian nationalism. He was Archibald's executive instrument in carrying out the policy of creating an Australian school of writers, and served this aim with a wholehearted energy. He was thus typical of Australian educated middle-class opinion in his responsiveness to the best European bourgeois culture of his day, and in his acceptance of its standards of judgment. He was distanced from that class by his championship of the emergent native writers.

Stephens is seldom at his best in discussing Lawson. There were probably personal strains between the two men. Stephens saw himself somewhat as the schoolmaster of Australian letters, striving to develop a sense of artistic refinement in writers handicapped by the cultural immaturity of their social environment. He often adopted a tone of pedagogic admonition. Lawson, permanently bitter over his failure to acquire an education, was quick to suspect and to resent condescensions from the learned. He complained to Brereton that "the Bulletin itself had reminded him of his 'lack of culture' till he was sick of it,"[13] and by "Bulletin" he probably meant "Stephens."

There is a grudging note in Stephens' early reviews of Lawson, although they give high praise, including the statement that his work had "a touch of genius." The grudging note is particularly apparent in Stephens' review of the *While the Billy Boils* volume in 1896. Most scholars of Australian literature would agree that this book was the finest artistic achievement which had appeared in Australia up to the time of its publication; yet Stephens begins his welcome to this epoch-making book with a column of complaint, some of it justified. He could fairly assert that the selections included too many bits of potboiling below Lawson's better level of writing; he could reasonably attack the sentimentality of some of the early pathetic stories, overinfluenced by Dickens at his worst. He showed less perception when he complained that this collection of short stories and sketches lacked continuity, and suggested that "Lawson might conceivably have written his fragmentary impressions into a single plotted climaxed story which would make a permanent mark." One can imagine no better way of destroying Lawson's delicacy of touch. One might as sensibly assert that Herrick's "Hesperides" is not an effective book because the poems are nearly all short, and that they should have been recomposed into an epic.

Stephens was at this stage an extreme exponent of the theory that Lawson was a "natural" without technical mastery. He roundly declares "Art he has none; his artifices are of the feeblest." The one point of value which the review makes is Stephens' recognition that sensitivity is the source of Lawson's success: "the trifles which make evanescent impressions on other minds draw blood (and ink) from his."[14] A later essay on Lawson, written after his death, shows Stephens exercising his critical talents more effectively and achieving a fuller appreciation of Lawson's work. In the *While the Billy Boils* review, Stephens condescendingly remarks, "His quaint simple style suits his themes and modes of thought." In his essay he shows a more positive sense of the virtues of that style:

> The simple graphic strength of Lawson's prose . . . would be remarkable in any literature. . . . Probably wider culture would have weakened his true force, his instinctive emphasis. There are other styles, probably better styles; but in its way, to its degree, Lawson's style is unsurpassed.[15]

Incidentally, one notes that Stephens' own style had improved and had drawn rather closer to Lawson's. The early review is marred by splurges of loose rhetoric. That blue pencil which was virtually Archibald's sixth finger must often have itched to get to work on the Literary Editor's copy. In the essay, Stephens writes more directly, and more consistently well. No doubt that is largely due to his personal maturing, but it also reflects a change in the standards governing the writing of English prose. Cultured readers now valued, even demanded, the kind of economic precision which Lawson had practiced at a time when it was regarded as lacking in elegance. Time had unexpectedly proved Lawson to be a literary pioneer.

The freer appreciation in this essay is still hedged about with a good many "buts." Stephens is now firmer than he had once been in recognizing the limitations of Lawson's verse: "He was no poet in the high sense, though the rhythmic energy of his verse is remarkable. . . . He wanted a sense of the melody of words; he felt their sonorous force, but not their inner harmony." He also now clearly defines what he regards as Lawson's disqualification from the higher levels of greatness: "In a characteristic valuation Lawson's work is a reliving of the facts of life; he had only a small capacity for associating ideas; he described people and scenes individually, without generalising, without rising to the symbol above the substance." It appears to be on this ground that, a little earlier in the essay, Stephens had said, "Much of his work remains to Australia; very little to the world." [16]

Stephens also continues to protest in this essay, as he always had, against the gloominess of Lawson's view. In the *Bulletin* review of Lawson's first book (apart from the volume which Louisa brought out), Stephens—if he is the writer of that review—is already complaining that the pessimistic note is being increasingly struck in Lawson's work: "The change of note from Hope to Discontent, the change of view from impersonal to personal, has not improved Lawson's work. The less he broods, the better he writes." [17]

The essay devotes what seems an excessive amount of space to attacks of the same kind. Stephens now takes the view that Lawson had a rare talent for seeing accurately and for truthfully rendering what he saw; but that the bias of his temperament so dictated what he looked at that the resultant picture was distorted:

> He could feel and he could see and he could write what he saw, and he wrote the truth. Which truth? The truth of his temperament and his knowledge and his misery. His lamentations rose to heaven like Jeremiah's, and they have done their share in misrepresenting that vast country Australia beyond the seas.[18]

The overemphasis which Stephens gave to this theme at first puzzled me. It seemed to me that a man with Stephens' understanding of the nature of the artistic process should have recognized the subjective compulsions which control the work of every artist of worth, and that he should have been more ready to accept them. I found a clue to a possible explanation when I confronted another puzzle. Stephens' essay begins rather unhappily. He declares that Lawson was "in character . . . typically an English peasant" [19] and elaborates this theme lengthily. It seems a silly conception. A quivering sensitivity was the source both of Lawson's artistic success and of his human unhappiness, as Stephens recognized; it is not a trait which one associates with the type of the English peasant. Nor are Stephens' positive arguments for his thesis convincing. Thus he quotes Lawson's lines:

> I wonder would the apathy of wealthy men endure,
> Were all their windows level with the faces of the poor?
> Ah! Mammon's slaves, your knees shall knock, your hearts in terror beat,
> When God demands a reason for the sorrows of the street.

Stephens comments: "That is old English village sentiment." [20] It seems a strange view of Chesterton's "Secret People."

I could not understand how such an acute mind came to talk such doctrinaire nonsense until I isolated this passage:

> The peasant character, the village attitude, were Lawson's English inheritance; they coloured his life in Australia: he saw Australia through an English glass darkly. His English personality was always at odds with this strange exotic environment. For much of his mind, much of his life, he was with us but not of us.[21]

The purpose of this passage seems unmistakable. Stephens is trying to depose Lawson from his generally accepted ranking as a "true Australian." He needed to do that because Lawson's gloomy interpretation of Australia clashed with the kind of national prides in which Stephens believed. As he felt it, Lawson was eroding the myth; therefore he had to be contraverted.

III *The Outside View*

Those few overseas writers who took any notice of Lawson were not, of course, affected by the misjudgments which appear in the early Australian assessments of his work, although the first Englishman of established literary repute who acclaimed Lawson was impressed by his verse-writing. Richard Le Gallienne devoted most of one of his literary causeries to a discussion of Lawson's first collection of ballads. Le Gallienne is, however, aware of a distinction which many of the early Australian commentators ignored, although he has trouble in defining it:

> I don't mean to imply that he is a poet of anything approaching the highest order of poetry. Ballad poetry has seldom been written by such poets. It is essentially music of the people, appealing to the great human emotions, not in the way great poets appeal to them but—but enough of criticism.[22]

At this point Le Gallienne rescues himself from the deep waters into which he has unwisely ventured by throwing himself a life-belt: he devotes most of the rest of the review to quotation from Lawson—over a hundred lines of it. One wonders if Lawson was flattered by the compliment or if he ruefully reflected that Le Gallienne was receiving the check for copy which his own pen had provided.

The first really perceptive criticism of Lawson's work was written by his helpful friend, Edward Garnett. Again, admiration from such a source seems at first surprising, for Garnett was one of the highbrows of his day. He was more accustomed to write of such favorites of the intelligentsia as Nietzsche, Ostrovsky, and Hudson. There was, however, another side to Garnett. More than most conscious esthetes of his day, he saw literature as primarily the communication of lived experience rather than as the creation of delicate and beautiful forms. He was an admirer of D. H. Lawrence long before that was a modish literary enthusiasm. He wrote a series of essays on American poetry at a time when most Englishman of the cultural establishment arched bored eyebrows at mention of the vulgar continent. It is thus not really surprising that Garnett was enthusiastic about the freshness of Lawson's stories. He dismissed the verse with a summary firmness which would have outraged the bushmen: "His verse, to put it bluntly, is the verse of a thousand and one vigorous versifiers of to-day . . . which shows the stamp of the literary artisan rather than that of the artist." [23] As one would expect, Garnett is most interested in Lawson's success in "democratizing" literature. Here was someone who produced what many progressive Englishmen were vainly seeking in their own literature—an interpretation of the working classes without condescension and with intimacy of understanding.

Garnett corrects the valuation which led many of the contemporary Australian commentators to assume Lawson's technical incompetence: "Lawson's journalistic sketches establish fresh creative values of life, but the merely ingenious story-tellers only reaffirm stale valuations." [24] He could not, however, entirely escape the influence of conventional esthetic expectations in judging Lawson. He writes: "Read 'The Union Buries Its Dead,' if you care to see how the most casual, 'newspapery' and apparently artless art of this Australian writer carries with it a truer, finer, more delicate commentary on life than do the idealistic works of any of our genteel school of writers." [25] This passage perceptively, and even boldly, recognizes a quality in Lawson which most readers with Garnett's kind of background would have missed; but certain hesitations reveal themselves. That word "artless" has again attached itself to Lawson. Perhaps Garnett intended the emphasis to rest on the accompanying "apparently." Even if this were so, his escape from genteel standards is not quite complete.

"Newspapery" is a strange term to apply to Lawson's writing. It is true that he was strongly influenced by the precepts of Archibald and by the style which the *Bulletin* had developed; but the *Bulletin* was no ordinary paper. Most English journals at that day still used a thumping rhetoric, a prose which flashed with tinselly ornament or measured out a pompous pseudo-gravity. Only a handful of the most responsible journalists were then attempting the simple directness which Lawson had mastered. I suspect that Garnett was led to that inappropriate word because in the vocabulary of the esthetes of his day, "journalistic" was the antonym of "literary." It was thus natural for him to use the term "newspapery" to define a lack of the refinements and graces of consciously ordered prose which he expected in writing worth taking seriously.

It is greatly to Garnett's credit that he could so far overcome prejudices very natural in a critic with his background; at least he understood that lack of the "genteel" qualities might be no disadvantage, might even be an advantage. The survival of such prejudices, however, weakens his final summing-up of Lawson:

> If Lawson's tales fail to survive in another fifty years—and where will be much of Kipling's, Stevenson's, Hardy's and Henry James's fiction then—it will be because they have too little beauty of form,

and there is too much crudity and roughness of form in their structure.[26]

At first sight that seems a fair criticism of the work of the untutored bushboy. Under closer inspection, it withers. Beauty of form may help the survival of poetry; but has it much to do with the lasting power of fiction? Russian readers complain of the crudity of Dostoevsky's prose, but they do not therefore question his genius; Balzac's hasty vitality has survived better than the exquisiteness of Flaubert. For the consumer of fiction, the pudding's proof is in the flavor not the shape. Garnett was, I think, right to feel that Lawson's work lacks the quality of assured and lasting greatness; but the false literary tenets of his environment prevented him from accurately diagnosing Lawson's limitations.

IV *Emile Saillens*

A more fully satisfying appraisal of Lawson came from Paris—about the last environment from which one would expect discerning praise of so unsophisticated a writer. Emile Saillens, a professor in the School of English at the Sorbonne, and the author of a distinguished book on Milton, had visited Australia, had there discovered Lawson's work and found in it an exciting expression of the qualities which the visitor felt in the country and its people. In 1911 he prepared a volume of his own translations of Lawson stories into French. Its introduction stands as one of the best criticisms of Lawson ever written.

Saillens was as little impressed by Lawson's verse as Garnett had been, but he was warier in expressing his opinion of it. He pointed out that it expressed Australian national aspirations, and he therefore felt that a Frenchman could not accurately assess its worth: "His verses . . . are accessible only by our intelligence, and the poetry whose pathos or joy of living we do not directly feel is a poetry reft of its subtlest charm."[27] On the subject of Lawson's mastery as a prose writer, Saillens showed none of the reservations felt by Garnett, and he explicitly rejects the Australian assumptions of Lawson's technical naïveté: "He is an artist not fully recognized as such by his Australian readers." He also speaks of the "perfection of his literary craftsmanship" and "the hidden might of his art."

Elsewhere Saillens shows a rather more perceptive response

than Garnett's, due partly, no doubt, to his knowledge of the life which Lawson depicts. Thus he remarks, with a nice precision, "Bushmen are nearly always the heroes, or rather the passive personages, of his unexcited stories." On Lawson's relation to his environment he says: "Lawson cannot be said to *love* the bush; yet any other environment is uncongenial to him. . . . Is it not the lover who hates his mistress and yet cannot live apart from her?" [28]

Perhaps a weakness appears in Saillens' treatment of Lawson's interpretation of the bush. He had obviously taken some trouble to discover the facts of Lawson's life, but it is unlikely that he knew of the importance of Lawson's relationship with his mother; in any case, a pre-Freudian might not have attached the importance to it that a modern does. Saillens is therefore tempted to assume that Lawson's melancholy was essentially a reflection of his environment, the more so because a European visitor's first impression of the bush is usually dominated by his sense of its melancholic, even oppressive, nature. Saillens' interpretation of the bush's influence on the bushmen accurately defines its effect on the European:

> He is oppressed by the silence, the immobility, the monotony of colour and form, the overhanging heat and glare of the great Australian wastes. These oceans of uniform shrubs without landmarks, where the stars or compass alone can serve as guides, these vast and mighty forests where water is found only by boring, where the sole living creatures are a few raucous or songless birds, a few elusive animals or lurking deadly serpents, constrain the most intrepid to discouragement, bitterness and a gloomy taciturnity.[29]

The view which Saillens there expresses and which harmonizes with the impression created by Lawson, was not the view commonly asserted by bushmen. For them the bush had the glow of home; its spaces were not terrifying because they knew the art of mastering them; and they were less oppressed by its grayness because they were not making comparisons with European greens.

And yet it may be that Saillens and Lawson more truly convey the bushmen's feelings than their own assertions do. The myth declared that the bushman was a careless optimist with faith in the future; but the melancholy which afflicted Lawson appears again and again in Australian writing. Was that simply because the artist's sensitivity responded to influences from the environment which the ordinary extrovert escaped? Or was it the artist's sense of truth penetrating to an influence which the extrovert felt but did not admit? Were the bushmen in their mythic assertions of optimism merely "cracking hardy," shrugging off the melancholy which afflicted them too, but which the naïveté of their national pride bade them deny? Perhaps Saillens was misled by his European standards of the normal; but perhaps he intuitively recognized in Lawson a form of typical Australian feeling which others suffered but would not admit, and in which Stephens found a betrayal of the *Bulletin* creed.

Despite Saillens' intense admiration of Lawson, he perceived the Australian writer's limitation more accurately than Garnett had. Saillens indicated the similarity between the work of Lawson and that of Gorki—a fairly obvious parallel (but its recognition shows a good deal more understanding than that displayed by the English publisher who labeled Lawson "the Australian O. Henry").[30] Having indicated Lawson's likenesses to the Russian, Saillens goes on to point out his main difference: "The Australian writer has seen and felt rather than formulated. Generalizations and abstractions are very rare with him." This points the way toward the limitation which keeps Lawson's work below the level of final greatness, as Stephens also had perceived (or, rather, was to perceive, since his essay came later than Saillens'). Saillens, however, hardly admits that Lawson was so limited and perhaps when he said that Lawson could not generalize, he was thinking of the lack of a more formal and less artistically limiting quality than Stephens had in mind. Saillens continues:

> Yet there is in his work abundant evidence of the spirit that makes the classics, a genuine comprehension of what is deeply and eternally human. This bent of mind, owing to the impersonal method of his art, is more easily felt than proved. . . . A man who knew nothing of Australia could still appreciate Lawson for the sake of his broad humanity.[31]

V *The Australian View Changes*

About the mid-1930's a new attitude began to assert itself in Australian self-assessments. The preceding decades had retreated from the confident independence of the 1890's. At that time Australian society had been bold in attempting sociopolitical experiments; but this impetus had lost much of its force, and Australians now tended to imitate English developments at a discreet distance rather than to develop their own ideas. As the great depression of the 1930's lifted, the Australian sense of independence reasserted itself. In particular, there was a voicing of demands for the development of an Australian cultural expression which would convey the special flavor of the community and which should no longer dutifully accept European cultural modes.

Those who declared these needs naturally found support for their attitude in the successful nationalistic literary movement of the nineties. The names "Lawson and Furphy" began increasingly to appear in Australian cultural discussions, usually as an integral phrase as inseparable as "bacon and eggs" or "Gilbert and Sullivan." These two had not only been probably the best prose writers whom the nation had produced, they had expressed a distinctively Australian point of view. They exemplified qualities which the champions of the new cultural nationalism wanted to revive, although these champions also hoped that the new movement would not repeat the brashness and artistic vulgarity of the old. Thus Lawson and Furphy began to assume the stature of Founding Fathers. Their work now seemed worth an alertness of critical examination which hitherto only Stephens had bestowed upon it.

The new cultural nationalism was not so closely allied to working-class loyalties as the old had been. Many of its leaders were members of the middle class with university training. Thus the new critical assessments of Lawson escaped the naïvetés of judgment which had affected the older attempts. This emerges most clearly in the approach of critics to two convenient testing points —the comparative valuation of Lawson's prose and his verse and the estimation of his technical skill.

The expressions of the new view of Lawson appear earlier than the date which I have arbitrarily fixed for the emergence of the new cultural nationalism, because some of the best critical expressions of the new approach came from pioneers who felt the need for it before it had begun to gather general support. Prominent among these pioneers was the husband-and-wife team of Vance and Nettie Palmer. The latter published a pamphlet on "Modern Australian Literature" as early as 1924. It gives a markedly different estimate of Lawson from that advanced two years earlier by Mrs. Cross. Mrs. Palmer gives only one (sympathetic) sentence to Lawson's poetry, but nearly two pages to his prose.[32] She rejects the old view of his technical naïveté, using an argument similar to that advanced by both Garnett and Bayldon:

> Lawson seems to have led the way to the real story in Australia. A real story is one whose writer believes in the subject, and wants to express it with the fullest truth and sincerity. The unreal story is one of mechanism only. . . . Lawson has too deep a respect for the life he described to falsify it for the sake of mechanical effects. . . . Although his stories are sometimes rough and defective in detail there is a fine freedom about their general form. Their loose, easy look is not due to limpness but to perfect control.

Vance Palmer did not publish his main developed view of Lawson until 1954, but the opinions he there expressed were probably developed long before. He was unimpressed by the verse: "It is undoubtedly in his stories that Lawson achieved his most durable work. . . . In his verse he was different, too cloudy in his ideas, often, to seek exact utterance." He repeats that word "artless" but with a clear understanding of its misleading nature: "With a seemingly artless simplicity he was able to get subtle and powerful effects." [33] Palmer does not feel the old need to contravert or to apologize for Lawson's melancholy, accepting it as a necessary part of his essentially subjective art:

> Drought held sway perpetually over the landscape of his mind. . . . There had been his experience of Pipeclay in his boyhood; later on he had spent a few months in the arid country around Bourke. Yet it is doubtful whether contact with a different background would have altered his point of view.[34]

H. M. Green expresses similar valuations; for once the term "artless" has been definitely rejected in his interpretation that "Lawson was by no means without Art," continuing with a view similar to that of Nettie Palmer: "He wrote one of those simple and natural and apparently casual styles that seem as easy as talking, but are not." [35] Unlike Palmer, Green does feel a need to defend Lawson against the charge of pessimism.[36] He bases his defense on the grounds that Lawson wrote many humorous stories—a ground which I would reject for reasons which I have already stated. This attitude seems to me a minor defect in one of the best of all assessments of Lawson's work.

Perhaps the shift of view in this generation of critics is best pointed for us in F. T. Macartney's revision of Morris Miller's Bibliography. Faced with Miller's use of the word "artless," Macartney—a far more perceptive reader than Miller—obviously feels that the term is unsatisfactory, and gives it, in his replacing comment, a juster gloss:

Lawson's writing is artless in the sense that it had its origin in a remarkable natural gift owing little to literary influences, and it is skilful in that the sure effects it achieves would not have been possible without careful constructive effort.[37]

The change in estimate which Lawson's verse had suffered can be illustrated with a mathematical precision not often attainable in such discussions. I append a table[38] showing the number of selections taken from the work of four poets in three Australian poetry anthologies, published in 1918, 1927, and 1956, respectively. The three names which follow Lawson's are those of the writers now generally considered the best poets in Australia during the early 1900's:

	1918	1927	1956
Lawson	3	1	1
Brennan	4	8	9
McCrae	3	8	8
Neilson	6	6	8

It will be observed that what the Australian critics of the 1930's had achieved was a view of Lawson closely similar to that held by Garnett and Saillens a generation earlier, but not at that time shared by Australian readers. This prophet had had plenty of honor in his own country, but it had not hitherto been judiciously rendered.

VI *The Pendulum Fails to Swing*

Toward the end of the 1950's the revived nationalism had ceased to dominate literary discussions in Australia. That was partly because it had largely achieved its main aim of creating a readiness of response to their own literature among cultured Australians; but there was also a positive reaction against many of the nationalist tenets.

In the short history of Australia as a culturally aware community, there has been a notable tendency for opinion to veer between two extremes. One generation will feel the need to assert Australia's "differentness," to encourage the production of a literature which will convey the special tone and flavor of the community, and which will develop the self-confidence which a youthful community of colonial origin finds hard to attain. The next generation is often dismayed by the crudity which a literature thus directed often displays; its members begin to wonder if isolation from the main sources of European cultural influence is not a graver danger to Australia than the lack of self-confidence and the consequent tendency to imitate. Thus there develops a rejection of the nationalist demands, and discussion begins to stress the need for Australian writers to learn by the study of the superior sophistication of Europe. In the late 1950's the pendulum swung toward this view. (It should be understood that the generalizations which I have used to indicate prevailing trends of opinion greatly oversimplify the situations which I discuss. Nationalist and antinationalist opinions existed side by side in all periods, and in a great variety of forms.)

How did this swing of the pendulum affect the readiness of response to Lawson's work, which had been so closely associated with the nationalist ideas? The interesting point here is that the new swing did not in the least weaken that response, even among the more vigorous antinationalists. They denied the validity of the Australian "tradition" in the form which, the nationalists claimed, it derived from the works of Furphy and Lawson; but they felt no desire to dethrone the Founding Fathers themselves. The estimate of Lawson accepted by most Australians remained that established by such critics as H. M. Green and the Palmers.

The work of C. Wallace-Crabbe illustrates this survival of Lawson's repute. Crabbe is a strong antinationalist; he has rebutted the claim that the natural trend for Australian writing today is a development, in modern terms, of the attitudes established by the *Bulletin* school. That rejection, however, did not prevent him from writing a sympathetic and sensitive study of Lawson which, for the first time, examined in detail the importance and the real nature of the *Joe Wilson* stories. He introduces his discussion with the assertion that Lawson's prose achievement stands "square and solid and unmistakable." [39] One observes, incidentally, that Lawson could now thus be discussed with complete propriety by a writer of Crabbe's type, a lecturer in a university school of English literature, and a poet responsive to current European influences. Even in the thirties, such an interest from such a quarter would have been considered an eccentricity.

Perhaps more striking evidence of the survival of Lawson's reputation is conveyed by the tendency of the antinationalists to claim his work as evidence for their own theories, rather than to see in it an exemplification of the type of Australianism based on the bushman myth. Thus Professor G. A. Wilkes, first occupant of a Chair of Australian Literature in an Australian University, has published an essay designed to correct the exaggerated importance with which the nationalists regarded the *Bulletin* school. He has little difficulty in showing that most members of that school were third-rate writers of no lasting importance. He does not, however, attempt to deny the value of the work of Lawson and Furphy; he prefers to fit them into his thesis by arguing that, in important respects, their work contradicts the doctrines of the *Bulletin* school. In Lawson's case, he bases his claim on the fact that Lawson expressed his Australianist convictions mainly in his verse. If this were the important element in his writing, Professor Wilkes suggests, his reputation would rest on his verse rather than on his prose.[40]

Dr. H. P. Heseltine is an even more audacious kidnapper (although he is not a strong antinationalist). Unlike the critics of earlier generations, he is not ill at ease in confronting Lawson's melancholy. On the contrary, he seizes on it as the basic element in Lawson's writing, the expression of his deepest intuitions about the nature of life. The element in his work which expresses the bushmen myth conceptions, Dr. Heseltine dismisses as superficial, drawn from shallower levels of Lawson's imagination, and used by him, in Dr. Heseltine's view, as a means of escape from the nihilism to which his intuitions led him but which he could not bear to face:

"It didn't matter much—nothing does." The assertion is shocking in its finality, but it is the (sometimes unacknowledged) burden of much of Lawson's best writing. If some of Lawson's stories seem rather thin, it is not because they were without content. Rather, they could not afford to face up to their true subject—nothing. They had to take refuge in sociability, they had to create some kind of face or personality which would make shift in the world; in short they had to opt for mateship.[41]

In my view, Dr. Heseltine's interpretation underestimates the importance of certain elements in Lawson's work and the force of conviction behind them. Nonetheless, it contains valid perceptions. It will incidentally be observed that this critic of the 1960's sees the element which Stephens regarded as Lawson's weakness as his strength, wishing that he had expressed it in a less compromised form; and that his views confirm the intuitions of Saillens.

Following a very different line from those I have been discussing, two recent writers have tried to restore the verse of Lawson to favor (neither of them is a bushman enthusiast). Dr. S. Murray-Smith writes of the adverse criticisms of Lawson as a poet, "such particularity chills the blood" and proceeds to argue an opposite view. Professor Colin Roderick follows similar lines, although his case is put with less cogency of argument and sensitiveness of literary response than Dr. Murray-Smith's.

I cannot pretend to judge this issue with impartiality, since I am cited by Dr. Murray-Smith as one of the blood-chilling particularists, and am also included in Professor Roderick's list of reprobates. Moreover, the issue cannot be usefully argued. It depends in the last resort on what one finds to be satisfactory poetry, and that is a matter of taste, incapable of logical assessment. I shall therefore present to the reader representative specimens of the evidence and leave him to make his own judgment. Dr. Murray-Smith writes:

There have been few more moving, dignified and poetically effective lines in our literature than

"In the shearers' hut the slush-lamp shows a haggard stern-faced man
Preaching war against the Wool-king to his mates;
And wherever go the billy, water-bag and frying-pan,
They are drafting future histories of state." [42]

If the reader finds these lines worthy of Dr. Murray-Smith's epithets, he should dismiss from his mind all the blood-chilling comments on Lawson's verse which I have made in this book. He and

I do not agree about the nature of poetry. Professor Roderick cites the following lines as evidence that Lawson commanded "the note of genuine poetry":

When the love-burst came, like an English spring,
In the days when our hair was brown,
And the hem of her skirt was a sacred thing
And her hair was an angel's crown.[43]

Either Professor Roderick is tone deaf to poetry, or I am.

In this brief review of Lawson criticism, I have preferred to emphasize the points about which there has been disagreement or a change of view. I have thus, perhaps, distorted the picture, since there are certain qualities which almost all critics in all periods have found in Lawson's work, and which lie near the heart of their admiration for him. Those qualities may perhaps best be summed up in a sentence written by H. M. Green: "Sympathy, and with that, simplicity and sincerity; these are the basic principles of Lawson's work." [44]

One should add one other specially important, and generally recognized, quality—the exceptional power which Lawson has to convey the feeling of Australia and of the Australians. His characters have a simple human universality; but they are nevertheless immediately recognizable, by those who know, as Australians; they could never be anything else.

Perhaps a personal experience may best convey the force of this power. Once, in the London home of an expatriate Australian friend, I found myself with an hour of loose time on my hands, and plucked a copy of *While the Billy Boils* from the bookshelves. I am a city-living Australian, and my country hikes have taken me more into the lovely scenery of the mountains than to the bare baked plains which Lawson best knew. By breeding and circumstance, I belong to the professional class and have made only chance, though cherished, contacts with the kind of men and women Lawson wrote about. Yet within half an hour of taking up that book, I was, for the only time in my life, hopelessly homesick. The tone, the flavor, almost the smell of Australia, had seeped from the book into my mind, reminding me how much a stranger I was in that prim London suburb.[45]

In the canon of Australian fiction, the names of Joseph Furphy, Henry Handel Richardson, and Patrick White must stand higher than Lawson's, by virtue of their greater stamina, range, and imaginative largeness; but none of them could have won that convincing tribute.

Notes and References

References to the stories of Lawson are to the collection, *The Stories of Henry Lawson,* edited by Cecil Mann (Sydney, 1964). The title of the work is abbreviated in the references to SHL, followed by Roman numerals to indicate whether the reference is to the first, second, or third series. (Mr. Mann uses the term "series" to distinguish the three volumes of his work.)

References to poems by Lawson are to *The Poetical Works of Henry Lawson,* with Preface and Introduction by David McKee Wright (Sydney, 1918; latest edition, 1964), unless the poem cited is not included in that work. The title of the book is abbreviated to PWL.

Where reference is made to *The* [Sydney] *Bulletin,* the title of that journal is abbreviated to *Bull.*

Chapter One

1. Vance Palmer, *The Legend of the Nineties* (Melbourne, 1954).
2. *The Webbs' Australian Diary,* edited by A. G. Austin (Melbourne, 1965), pp. 113–15.
3. SHL, II, p. 160.
4. Marnie Masson, *The Hentys* (Oxford, 1954), p. 186.
5. Joseph Furphy, *Such Is Life* (Sydney, 1943), pp. 39–41.
6. J. F. Archibald, "The Genesis of the Bulletin," *The Lone Hand,* May 1907, p. 54.
7. Bertha Lawson, *My Henry Lawson* (Sydney, 1945), p. 134.
8. "A Sketch of Archibald," SHL III, p. 413.
9. Archibald's high standard of factual accuracy here deserts him. Lawson was, in 1887, twenty, not seventeen. Archibald's recognition of Lawson's talent may have been helped by his knowledge that the youngster had the potentially valuable gift of persistence; Lawson had first submitted verse to *The Bulletin* several months earlier. It had been rejected, but "Answers to Correspondents" had bidden him keep on trying. He had settled to a careful revision of his poem and resubmitted it. Again it was rejected, with encouraging comment; again Lawson squared his elbows and worked at its improvement—this time with success.

Chapter Two

Any biographical account of Lawson must be considerably indebted to the only full-scale work on his life, Denton Prout's *Henry Lawson, the Grey Dreamer* (Adelaide, 1963).

1. SHL I, p. 32. This passage comes from an account of his early life written by Lawson at the instigation of George Robertson, unpublished until many years after Lawson's death.
2. SHL I, p. 32.
3. Gertrude O'Connor, *Notes upon the Personal Life of Henry Lawson,* a manuscript deposited in the Mitchell Library, Sydney.
4. PWL, p. 82.
5. Quoted by John Tierney in "Lawson's Eurunderee," SHL III, p. 522.
6. See "A Fragment of Autobiography," SHL I, p. 16, and "Joe Wilson's Courtship," SHL II, p. 16.
7. See "Grandfather's Courtship," SHL III, p. 3.
8. From an interview published in *Bull.*, 1896, quoted in SHL III, p. 103.
9. From MS notes on her life by Louisia Lawson, in the Mitchell Library.
10. MS by Gertrude O'Connor, *op. cit.*
11. SHL I, p. 9.
12. J. W. Gordon, *Under Wide Skies* (Leeton, 1947), p. 201.
13. SHL I, p. 28.
14. SHL I, p. 16.
15. SHL I, p. 22.
16. SHL I, p. 33.
17. Letter from Emma Brooks to J. F. Thomas, in the Mitchell Library.
18. SHL III, p. 29.
19. "Arvie Aspinall's Alarm-Clock," "Jones's Alley," and "Two Boys at Grinder Brothers" (SHL I, pp. 112, 224, and 417).
20. Gertrude O'Connor, MS.
21. See " 'Pursuing Literature' in Australia," SHL III, p. 399.
22. SHL II, p. 4.
23. SHL II, p. 3.
24. *Henry Lawson and His Mates,* ed. by Bertha Lawson and J. Le Gay Brereton (Sydney, 1931), p. 51.
25. " 'Pursuing Literature' in Australia," SHL III, p. 400.
26. "Bourke," PWL, p. 134.
27. *My Henry Lawson, op. cit.*
28. "Written Afterwards," PWL, pp. 60–61.
29. Some commentators attribute the composition of the *Joe Wilson* stories, perhaps Lawson's finest achievement, to this period. In so

doing they are following a statement made by Bertha Lawson (*My Henry Lawson*, p. 60), but her memory is probably at fault. Lawson says that "Brighten's Sister-in-law" was the first written of this series, and that story was based on an incident which occurred during one of Jim Lawson's attacks of convulsions (see p. 114). Jim was not born until after the Lawsons left Mangamaunu.

30. SHL III, p. 404.
31. *The Auld Shop and the New* (Sydney, 1923).
32. *Ibid.*, p. 25. Robertson included his own comments when he privately circulated this little volume.
33. Letter from Lawson to Emma Brooks, in the Mitchell Library.
34. In Beauchamp's Letter books for 1899, in the Mitchell Library.
35. *Henry Lawson by His Mates.*
36. PWL, p. 48.
37. "After All," PWL, p. 65.
38. E. J. Brady reports this—see SHL III, p. 499.
39. *Blackwoods* issued two volumes, one a reprint of earlier stories. Methuen also issued a volume of stories and verse.
40. *Henry Lawson by His Mates*, p. 114.
41. "The Last Review," PWL, p. 184.
42. SHL III, p. 485.
43. "Break o' Day," PWL, p. 158.
44. "A Foggy Night in Antwerp," SHL III, pp. 200–201.
45. *My Henry Lawson*, p. 79.
46. "The Man Who Died," SHL III, p. 285.
47. SHL III, p. 487. Many of the personal accounts of Lawson refer to similar incidents. One of David Low's caricatures shows Lawson holding three fingers aloft.
48. See "The Reformation of Johnson" (SHL III, p. 289) and "Sticking to Bill," PWL, p. 136.
49. See "The Songs They Used to Sing," SHL I, p. 265.
50. PWL, p. 32.
51. *Henry Lawson, the Grey Dreamer*, p. 256.
52. See "The Unknown God at Narrandera," SHL III, p. 324.
53. *Henry Lawson by His Mates*, p. 26.
54. There is a copy of the memorial in a MS, "The Hon. T. D. Mutch and His Work," in the Mitchell Library.
55. *Henry Lawson by His Mates*, p. 152.
56. SHL III, p. 505.
57. Personal information from Mr. Frank Hardy.

Chapter Three

1. Personal information from the late Vance Palmer.
2. SHL I, p. 324.

3. *The Collected Verse of A. B. Paterson,* with an Introduction by Frederick T. Macartney (Sydney, 1965), p. 10.
4. Quoted from an article in the *Sydney Morning Herald,* by Denton Prout in *Henry Lawson, the Grey Dreamer,* p. 103.
5. SHL I, p. 34.
6. "Up the Country," PWL, p. 78.
7. "In Defence of the Bush," *Collected Verse of A. B. Paterson,* p. 207.
8. "The Overflow of Clancy," by H. H. C. C., *Bull.,* August 20, 1892.
9. SHL II, p. 161.
10. SHL II, p. 150.
11. SHL I, p. 102.
12. PWL, p. 31.
13. "The Last Review," PWL, p. 183.
14. SHL I, p. 179.
15. SHL II, p. 153.
16. SHL I, p. 137.
17. SHL II, p. 151.
18. SHL II, p. 392.
19. PWL, p. 44.
20. SHL II, p. 12.
21. *Ibid.,* p. 24.
22. SHL II, p. 413.
23. "Joe Wilson in England," SHL III, p. 194, and "Grimy Old Babylon," SHL III, p. 404.
24. PWL, p. 117.
25. "A Stroll to the Strand," SHL III, p. 186.
26. "Madame Bong Fong," SHL III, p. 373.
27. In a poem on the Eureka Stockade (*Bull.,* March 2, 1889), Lawson wrote "I hear the broken English in the mouth at least of one" (of the rebels). The line has been altered in McKee Wright's edition of the poem, presumably by the editor, who was free with his emendations (see PWL, p. 118). This seems like a reference to Peter Larsen. In "An Old Mate of Your Father's" (SHL I, p. 76), Lawson describes the "father" and the "old mate" hushedly reminiscing about Eureka. The general basis for this sketch is Lawson's recollection of the old miners who used to visit his father, but of course any particular incident which he mentions may be fictitious.
28. SHL I, p. 46.
29. " 'Pursuing Literature' in Australia," SHL III, p. 398.
30. See "In Answer to Banjo and Otherwise," *Bull.,* August 6, 1892.
31. *Bull.,* June 18, 1892.
32. PWL, p. 5.

33. *The Sydney Worker,* May 1891.
34. SHL I, p. 49.
35. PWL, p. 105.
36. PWL, p. 2.
37. Lawson denied that he was influenced in his verse writing by Kipling, pointing out truthfully that he entered that field earlier than Kipling. "The Star of Australasia," however, has certain qualities stylistically which are not apparent in Lawson's earlier verse, and which strongly suggest Kipling's "The English Flag."
38. "When the World Was Wide," PWL, p. 50.
39. "Sydney in the Golden Nineties," SHL III, p. 111.

Chapter Four

1. "Hungerford," SHL I, p. 95.
2. "A Rough Shed," SHL I, p. 328.
3. "At Dead Dingo," SHL II, p. 147.
4. "The Romance of the Swag," SHL II, p. 191.
5. "Joe Wilson's Courtship," SHL II, p. 22.
6. SHL I, p. 196.
7. *The Australian Tradition* (Melbourne, 1958), p. 8.
8. "Joe Wilson's Courtship," SHL II, p. 2.
9. "Water Them Geraniums," SHL II, p. 47.
10. "They Wait on the Wharf in Black," SHL I, p. 415.
11. "The Union Buries Its Dead," SHL I, p. 119.
12. "Barney, Take Me Home Again," SHL II, p. 223.
13. "A Hero in Dingo Scrubs," SHL II, p. 166. This passage is not a fully satisfactory illustration of my point. It is not an incidental comment made by Lawson, but a piece of dialogue illustrative of the character of Doc Wilde.
14. "An Answer to Various Bards," *Collected Verse of A. B. Paterson,* p. 214.
15. SHL I, p. 232.
16. "The Story of the Oracle," SHL I, p. 434.
17. SHL I, p. 373.
18. Doc Wilde's most important appearances are in "A Hero in Dingo Scrubs" (SHL II, p. 160) and "Middleton's Peter" (SHL I, p. 288).
19. Peter M'Laughlin appears in " 'Shall We Gather at the River,' " "His Brother's Keeper," and "The Story of Gentleman Once," SHL II, pp. 238–70.
20. SHL II, pp. 138–39.
21. *Henry Lawson by His Mates,* p. 40.
22. SHL I, p. 119.
23. SHL I, pp. 122–23.

24. SHL II, p. 75.
25. SHL II, p. 104 and SHL I, p. 313.
26. "Baldy Thompson," SHL I, p. 247.
27. SHL II, p. 61.
28. J. Le Gay Brereton, *Knocking Around* (Sydney, 1930), p. 33.
29. SHL I, p. 112.

Chapter Five

1. Earl Beauchamp's Letter books, 1899, in the Mitchell Library.
2. SHL I, p. 108.
3. SHL II, p. 26.
4. The writers quoted are Hardy, Kipling, O. Henry, and A. Conan Doyle—a fair selection of Lawson's more successful contemporaries (O. Henry is a little later), avoiding more mannered writers such as James, Wilde, or Stevenson. The selection chosen is the first which came to hand in each case. Lawson may have learned something of the art of easy opening from Bret Harte, who practiced it skilfully.
5. The opening of the first three stories in *The Chorus Girl and Other Stories* (London, 1920), a selection in a series translated by Constance Crutt.
6. SHL II, p. 160.
7. SHL I, p. 294.
8. SHL I, p. 300.
9. SHL I, pp. 137–38.
10. *Henry Lawson: Twenty Stories and Seven Poems,* selected by Colin Roderick (Sydney, 1947).
11. "A Sketch of Archibald," SHL III, p. 412.
12. SHL II, p. 40.
13. PWL, p. 234.
14. SHL II, pp. 54–55.
15. SHL II, p. 75
16. SHL II, p. 24.
17. "The Babies in the Bush," *Bull.*, December 8, 1900.

Chapter Six

1. This view appears to be contradicted by the fact that the Australian Edition of *The Review of Reviews* published a criticism of Lawson's first book of verse, written by Professor E. E. Morris who held the chair of English at Melbourne University. Morris' article, however, shows a strong distaste for the prevailing type of Australian poetry and for Lawson's book. A few words of condescending praise sometimes break its general tone of disapproval.

Since this was a book of verse and since Lawson's ballads have seldom appealed much to the sophisticated, Morris' attitude is not surprising. It is more significant that he had apparently never heard of Lawson until he was asked to write the review. An Australian leader of literary opinion should certainly have known by that date (April 1896) that a short story writer of rare quality had appeared on the local literary scene.

In modification of my view, however, it should be noted that W. H. Fitchett, editor of the Australian Edition of *The Review of Reviews,* was certainly a representative of "middle-class culture" and that he had thought it worth seeking an authoritative review of Lawson's book. When *While the Billy Boils* appeared, he again gave good space to a review of it, this time in an enthusiastic tone (August 1896).

2. Joseph Jones, *The Union Buries Its Dead: Henry Lawson Commemorative Gathering Number Thirty-nine* (Hong Kong, 1965), p. 9.
3. See *Bull.*, Red Page, June 27, 1896.
4. J. M. Neild, *Lawson and His Critics* (Sydney, 1944).
5. Zora Cross, *An Introduction to the Study of Australian Literature* (Sydney, 1922), p. 62.
6. *Ibid.*, p. 56.
7. *The Poems of Bernard O'Dowd: Collected Edition* (Melbourne, 1941), p. 14.
8. *The Lone Hand,* I (August 1907), p. 451.
9. E. M. Miller, *Australian Literature 1810–1936* (Melbourne, 1940), pp. 466–70.
10. *Bull.*, January 18, 1910.
11. *Bull.*, February 3, 1910.
12. *Bull.*, December 23, 1909.
13. *Henry Lawson by His Mates,* p. 71.
14. *Bull.*, Red Page, August 29, 1896.
15. SHL III, p. 511. Stephens' essay originally appeared in *Art in Australia,* November 1922.
16. *Ibid.*, p. 510.
17. *Bull.*, Red Page, February 15, 1896. The article is unsigned, and Stephens was not then officially the paper's Literary Editor; but he did write most of the book reviews, and the style suggests his hand.
18. SHL III, p. 508.
19. *Ibid.*, p. 506.
20. *Ibid.*, p. 507.
21. *Ibid.*, p. 506.
22. "Wanderings in Bookland," *The Idler,* August 1896.
23. *Friday Nights* (London, 1922), p. 177. The essay is dated 1902.
24. *Ibid.*, pp. 178–79.
25. *Ibid.*, p. 183.

26. *Ibid.*, p. 186.

27. I have here used Saillens' own translation of the Introduction, published under the title of "The Discovery of Australia by France" in *The Lone Hand*, 1909. This passage occurs on p. 236. Saillens also wrote an essay on Lawson called "Le Bush Australien et Son Poéte" for *Le Mercure de France*, October 1910.

28. *Ibid.*, p. 240.

29. *Ibid.*

30. In 1924, Jonathan Cape republished *While the Billy Boils* in the Traveller's Library. This statement appears in the book's "blurb."

31. *The Lone Hand, op. cit.*, p. 239.

32. Nettie Palmer, *Modern Australian Literature* (Melbourne, 1924), pp. 9–11 and p. 24.

33. *The Legend of the Nineties* (Melbourne, 1954), p. 114.

34. *Ibid.*, p. 115.

35. H. M. Green, *Outline of Australian Literature* (Melbourne and Sydney, 1930), p. 114. I have preferred to quote from this work rather than from Green's fuller *History of Australian Literature* (Sydney, 1962) because the earlier book better indicates when Green formed his views. The writing of the *History* occupied him during several decades.

36. *History of Australian Literature, op. cit.*, p. 537.

37. E. M. Miller, *Australian Literature: A Bibliography to 1938*, extended to 1950 by Frederick T. Macartney (Sydney, 1956), p. 283.

38. *The Oxford Book of Australasian Verse,* chosen by Walter Murdoch (Oxford, 1918); *An Australasian Anthology* (*Australian and New Zealand Poems*), selected by Perceval Serle, assisted by Frank Wilmot and Robert E. Croll (London, 1927); *A Book of Australian Verse,* selected with an Introduction by Judith Wright (Melbourne, 1956).

39. Chris Wallace-Crabbe, "Lawson's *Joe Wilson:* A Skeleton Novel," *Australian Literary Studies,* June 1964, p. 147.

40. G. A. Wilkes, "The Eighteen Nineties," *Australian Literary Criticism,* ed. by Grahame Johnston (Melbourne, 1962), p. 37.

41. H. P. Heseltine, "The Literary Heritage," *Meanjin Quarterly,* No. 1, 1962, p. 42.

42. S. Murray-Smith, *Henry Lawson* (Melbourne, 1962), p. 35.

43. Professor Colin Roderick, *Henry Lawson: Poet and Short Story Writer* (Sydney, 1966), p. 27.

44. H. M. Green, *Outline of Australian Poetry,* p. 115.

45. H. M. Green apparently had a similar experience. *Cf.* the *Outline,* p. 115: "For an Australian to read him in another country is to breathe the air of home."

Selected Bibliography

PRIMARY SOURCES

A. Henry Lawson's Works (in chronological order)

Stories in Prose and Verse (Sydney, 1894). This is the booklet printed on Louisa Lawson's press.

In the Days When the World Was Wide and Other Verses (Sydney: Angus and Robertson, 1896).

While the Billy Boils (Sydney: Angus and Robertson, 1896). A collection of prose stories and sketches.

On the Track and Over the Sliprails (Sydney: Angus and Robertson, 1900). A collection of prose stories.

Verses, Popular and Humorous (Sydney: Angus and Robertson, 1900).

The Country I Came From (Edinburgh and London: Wm. Blackwood, 1901). This is a reprint of stories which were included in earlier volumes; its purpose was to introduce them to English readers.

Joe Wilson and His Mates (Edinburgh and London: Wm. Blackwood, 1901). Prose stories. An Australian edition was published by Angus and Robertson in the following year.

Children of the Bush (London: Methuen, 1902). A mixture of prose and verse.

When I Was King and Other Verses (Sydney: Angus and Robertson, 1905).

The Rising of the Court (Sydney: Angus and Robertson, 1910). Prose stories.

The Skyline Riders and Other Verses (Sydney: Fergusson, 1910).

A Coronation Ode and Retrospect (Sydney: Cofill, 1911).

Mateship, a Discursive Yarn (Melbourne: Lothian, 1911).

The Stranger's Friend (Melbourne: Lothian, 1911). A single story.

Triangles of Life and Other Stories (Melbourne: Strand Publishing Company, 1913).

For Australia and Other Poems (Melbourne: Strand Publishing Company, 1913).

My Army! O My Army! and Other Songs (Sydney: Tyrell's, 1915).

Selected Poems of Henry Lawson, with a Preface by David McKee Wright (Sydney: Angus and Robertson, 1918). Wright edited this collection.

The Auld Shop and the New. This is the set of verses about their relationship which Lawson sent to George Robertson. In 1923, Robertson had a few copies of the verses printed (with comments added by himself) and distributed to friends.

(Some volumes which only reprint material included in earlier volumes are omitted from the above list.)

B. Collected Editions

The best general collection of Lawson's prose is *The Stories of Henry Lawson,* edited by Cecil Mann (Sydney: Angus and Robertson, 1964). It includes all the stories which Lawson chose to include in volumes published with his authority, a number of other stories and articles taken from the files of periodicals, and the fragment of autobiography which Lawson wrote for George Robertson. Mr. Mann also includes six commentaries on Lawson written by six men who knew him (the classification is slightly strained to include H. M. Green, who thought that a stranger who once talked to him in a train was probably Lawson). The publication also includes commentaries on the stories by the editor, written in a gossipy and discursive style, but based on a thorough knowledge of Lawson's background.

The only easily available collection of Lawson's verse is *Poetical Works of Henry Lawson* (Sydney: Angus and Robertson, 1964). This is a reprint of the *Selected Poems* of 1918. It is not a very satisfactory volume: the poems are not arranged in chronological order, and they are not dated. Wright often makes his own emendations of the original texts, and his changes are not always improvements.

The reader who desires to familiarize himself with Lawson's best work, without making a full study of his writing, should read the stories contained in the volumes *While the Billy Boils* and *Joe Wilson and His Mates.* This material is, of course, contained in Mr. Mann's collection and can there readily be identified from the contents list. The separate volumes are no longer in print.

SECONDARY SOURCES

A. Select List of Material of Biographical Interest

The only full biography of Lawson is Denton Prout, *Henry Lawson, the Grey Dreamer* (Adelaide: Rigby, 1963). The book lacks literary expertise, but it is well researched and its interpretations are sensible and well balanced.

The most useful other sources of information are:

BERTHA LAWSON, *My Henry Lawson* (Sydney: Frank Johnson, 1943).

BERTHA LAWSON and J. LE GAY BRERETON (eds.), *Henry Lawson by His Mates*. This is a series of reminiscences by friends of Lawson. It tends to be overeulogistic in tone, but it contains much useful information and shows Lawson from widely varied points of view.

PROFESSOR COLIN RODERICK, *Henry Lawson's Formative Years 1883–1893* and *The Later Years of Henry Lawson* (Sydney: Wentworth Press, 1960). Two pamphlets containing material not elsewhere available.

MSS available in the Mitchell Library, Sydney, by Louisa Lawson (Henry's mother), Gertrude O'Connor (his sister), and Emma Brooks (his aunt).

B. Select List of Critical Material

GARNETT, EDWARD. "Henry Lawson and the Democracy," *Friday Nights* (London: Jonathan Cape, 1922). For comment, see p. 132.

GREEN, H. M. *History of Australian Literature* (Sydney: Angus and Robertson, 1962), pp. 532–51. A very well-balanced and discerning study.

HESELTINE, H. P. "The Literary Heritage," *Meanjin Quarterly*, No. 1, 1962, pp. 35–49. Only a few pages of this essay are devoted to Lawson, but they present an interesting point of view.

MURRAY-SMITH, STEVEN *Henry Lawson* (Melbourne: Landsdowne Press, 1961). This pamphlet gives about equal space to biographical and critical discussion: a satisfying general picture.

PALMER, VANCE. *National Portraits* (Sydney: Angus and Robertson, 1940), and *The Legend of the Nineties* (Melbourne University Press, 1954). Each of these volumes contains a short study of Lawson, sensitively considered and setting him against the background of his period.

SAILLENS, EMILE. "The Discovery of Australia by France," *The Lone Hand*, 1909, pp. 236 *et seq*., and "Le Bush Australien et Son Poéte," *Le Mercure de France*, October 1910. For comment, see p. 132.

STEPHENS, A. G. "Henry Lawson," *Art in Australia*, November 1922. For comment, see p. 127.

WALLACE-CRABBE, CRIS. "Lawson's *Joe Wilson:* A Skeleton Novel," *Australian Literary Studies*, June 1964, pp. 147–64. A close study of a key work of Lawson's.

Fuller details about the available material may be obtained by consulting George Mackaness, *An Annotated Bibliography of Henry Lawson* (Sydney: Angus and Robertson, 1951) and the extensive bibliography in Denton Prout's biography of Lawson.

Index

(References to Lawson's works will be found under the author's name.)